IRON CHANCELLOR

OTTO VON BISMARCK

Born: April 1, 1815
Died: July 30, 1898

Until he was thirty, Bismarck showed little ability as student, government clerk or soldier. Then, with his first taste of political power, his destiny became clear. The task he set hmself was enormous: to unify Germany under a Prussian monarch, at a time when she was hopelessly divided, the Prussian king was weak and liberalism was on the rise. By 1871 Bismarck saw William I crowned Emperor of Germany, and himself appointed Chancellor. Now the man who had based his policy on "blood and iron" designed a peace that lasted forty years. But even this master political magician could not prevent the death of the old Emperor and the crowning of a headstrong new ruler; and the man who had guided Germany to greatness was forced to spend his last years out of office, helplessly watching his life's work being undone.

IRON CHANCELLOR

Otto von Bismarck

by Alfred Apsler

Maps

JULIAN MESSNER   NEW YORK

Published simultaneously in the United States and Canada by
Julian Messner, a division of Simon & Schuster, Inc.,
1 West 39 Street, New York, N.Y. 10018. All rights reserved.

Printed in the United States of America
Library of Congress Catalog Card No. 68-25094

CONTENTS

IRON CHANCELLOR

OTTO VON BISMARCK

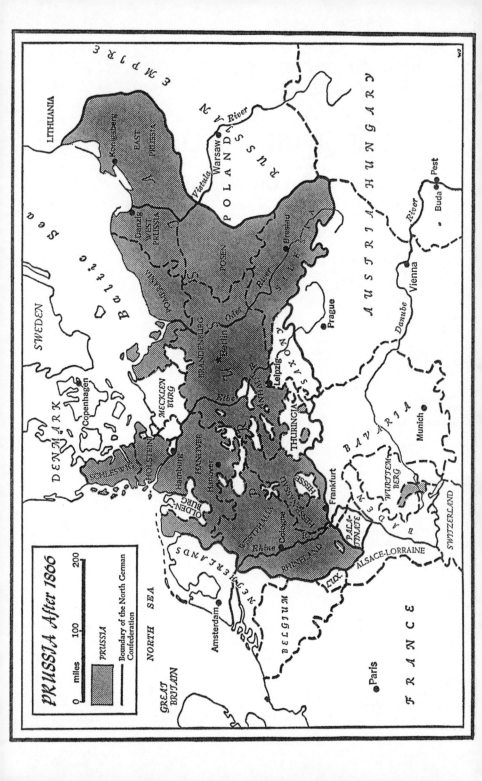

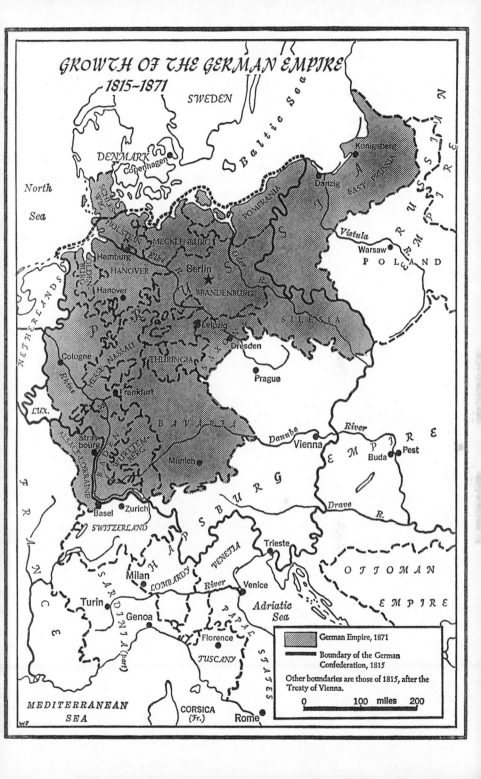

GROWTH OF THE GERMAN EMPIRE
1815–1871

SWEDEN

Baltic Sea

DENMARK
Copenhagen

North
Sea

SCHLESWIG
HOLSTEIN
MECKLENBURG
Hamburg
HANOVER
Hanover
Berlin
BRANDENBURG
POMERANIA
Oder R.
Elbe
Königsberg
EAST PRUSSIA
Danzig
P R U S S I A
Vistula
Warsaw
P O L A N D
R U S S I A N   E M P I R E

NETHERLANDS

LUX.

Cologne
HESSE-NASSAU
Rhine
Frankfurt
P R U S S I A
Leipzig
THURINGIA
Dresden
SILESIA
Prague

ALSACE-LORRAINE
Strasbourg
BADEN
WÜRTTEM-BERG
BAVARIA
Munich
Danube
River
Vienna
Buda
Pest

Basel   Zurich
SWITZERLAND

H A B S B U R G   E M P I R E

Drave
River
R.

FRANCE

SARDINIA (part)

Milan
LOMBARDY
VENETIA
River
Venice
Turin
Genoa
Trieste
Adriatic
Sea

OTTOMAN

E M P I R E

PAPAL STATES
Florence
TUSCANY

MEDITERRANEAN
SEA

CORSICA
(Fr.)
Rome

	German Empire, 1871
	Boundary of the German Confederation, 1815

Other boundaries are those of 1815, after the Treaty of Vienna.

0   100   miles   200

W?

SAD JUNKER

ON THE SWAYING QUARTERDECK OF THE BRITISH SHIP *Bellerophon* stood a small solitary figure. Napoleon, the terror of the battlefields, shivered under his olive-green greatcoat. This was the end. His eyes were nearly shut under the dark bushy eyebrows as he stared toward the fading outlines of the European continent which had lain conquered at his feet only a short time ago.

Clouds covered the sun. The sky was gray and cheerless as it had been on that day at Waterloo where he lost his last battle. Ahead lay the empty existence of a prisoner exiled to a desolate island somewhere in mid-ocean.

The enemy ship with the former emperor on board churned through the angry white-capped breakers of the English Channel. What thoughts were going through his mind? What does a man think about who has just lost the mightiest empire in the world?

Could he have wondered who would be the next great puppeteer on the puppet theater of history? Would there ever again be a man who could dictate to princes and shuffle nations like a deck of cards, as he had done? When would another giant set armies marching all over Europe once more, or quiet the guns when it suited his purpose? Who would be the next grand champion in the sport of all sports, the quest of political power?

The French conqueror, in his moment of deepest tragedy, could not possibly have known that such a person was already alive and breathing. He was a tiny baby, born only four months earlier, on April 1, 1815. Not that this child was to grow into another Napoleon. Greatness does not produce exact carbon copies. No, this child would grow up to become an architect with his own blueprint of the international scene.

In the nursery the windows were tightly closed to shut out dangerous fresh air, but through the small double panes of glass nodded the branches of majestic oak trees.

A chambermaid burst into the room. "Quick, Trine. The *Gnädige Frau* [gracious lady] wants to see the baby."

Nervously the nurse lifted the little bundle from the cradle and rushed to the parlor, a stuffy room with straight-backed oaken chairs and heavy curtains which admitted only dim shafts of sunlight.

With a disgusted wailing little Otto protested this disturbance of his sleep.

"The worst is over, thank God. He is recovering from the colic," said Frau Wilhelmine von Bismarck, as she hugged the baby to her breast. She was a finely built woman with a delicate face. The wrinkles on her high forehead formed a slender spiderweb. "If we can only nurse him through the first year, he will be all right."

She had reason to worry. Her older son was hale and strong, but two other children had died in infancy, a not uncommon fate in those days.

"Oh, he is a healthy rascal," bellowed the father good-naturedly. "A voice like a trumpet. Yesterday when I came back from the hunt, I could hear him scream long before I could even see the house."

Ferdinand von Bismarck, simple, rough and endowed with an enormous bulk, ruled almost absolutely over Schönhausen, one of his inherited landed estates east of the Elbe River. There Otto was born. When he was barely one year old, they moved to the Kniephof, another of the Bismarck holdings. It was a sprawling expanse of fields and forests in the heart of Pomerania, a province of Prussia.

Otto survived this and other illnesses. Everybody noticed how tall he was for his age. Countless freckles framed a pair of piercing blue eyes over which hung an unruly mop of red hair. With his brother

Bernhard, who was five years older, he roamed his father's diminutive kingdom. They wandered over yellow barley fields and tramped through the green patches formed by the leaves of sugar beets and potatoes. Sheep lazed on the wildflower-strewn meadows. Beyond the cultivated land, the dark forest rolled in gentle waves endlessly into the distance.

Outside the walls of the parklike garden clustered the peasant huts with their straw-thatched roofs, low and dirty-brown, almost like the sheep in the meadow. From the open shed which served as the blacksmith shop rose the clanging of metal on metal, and a strong odor drifted from the primitive distillery where potatoes were being converted into a cheap, but potent drink.

In the yard behind the master house chattered geese and ducks. They wandered in and out of the carriage sheds and stables, picking among the straw on the ground.

Otto stepped into one of the stables. A groom in muddy boots, gnarled and bent with age, tended the horses. With a knotty hand the old man swept the greasy cap from his head. "Good morning, Herr Junker. Want to see the colt? The big spotted mare dropped it last night."

"Sure, Klaas. Take me to her stall right away."

Hardly able to walk, the youngster already knew his place in the Prussian caste system. He called the old man by his first name and addressed him with the familiar *du* (thou). This was his privilege as a child of noble ancestry, while the keeper of the horses was the son and grandson of serfs. Though serfdom had been legally abolished a few years ago, Klaas was still not much more than a human possession of the family which owned the land and controlled the lives of the people who worked it.

Otto was a Junker, a member of the peculiar Prussian aristocracy, often denounced as overbearing, stubborn and hidebound, but sometimes also grudgingly admired as courageous, honest and dedicated to duty as long as this duty did not interfere with their inherited privileges.

As fortune-seeking warriors, Otto's ancestors had crossed the Elbe

River from the west over six hundred years ago. The Slavic tribes which stood in their way had been conquered and pressed into servitude. Huge estates of flat virgin land were the prizes of victory. To that land they became deeply attached, and like so many rural Europeans, they developed a strongly conservative frame of mind.

Despite the almost complete power over their peasants, the Junkers lived rather primitive lives. The Kniephof offered little of the refined luxuries found in the châteaux of the French aristocracy or on the stately English country seats. The Bismarcks were not above lending a hand with the farm chores to set a good example. They relaxed by hunting in the marshes or by visits to neighboring estates. Hearty eating and drinking were the main entertainment on such occasions.

Otto's family occupied the lowest rung on the aristocratic ladder. Only the simple *von* in front of the family name distinguished them from the gray mass of commoners. They had no other title, such as baron, count or prince. Yet on their estates they ruled like God's own personal representatives.

In the Reformation period of the sixteenth century, they had all become staunch Protestants. The Lutheran faith had been accepted as a matter of course without any brooding over its deeper meaning. Now when the bells of the unadorned village church tolled for Sunday prayers, the Bismarcks had themselves driven the short distance in their best carriage. Humbly the pastor conducted them to the special hand-carved oaken pews where they worshipped, splendidly isolated from their low-born coreligionists.

Practically all the male members of the clan had fought in the innumerable wars to which their state had been a party. Whatever conflict arose, Prussia's location at the halfway point between east and west involved the state almost automatically in the warfare. The Junker class had a monopoly on army commissions, from the lowliest lieutenant to the gold-bedecked field marshal. But Otto's father only served the barest minimum of time as an officer. He was a rare exception among his saber-rattling peers. While still in his early twenties, he had taken off the uniform and retired to the unexciting life of a country squire, his mind absorbed in the prices of wool and in the number of stags on his game preserve. Not even the tramping of Napoleon's regiments across Prussian soil could rouse him from his dull little world.

How this aristocratic simpleton could court and win his wife would be incomprehensible in any other social setting. Wilhelmine was a highly sensitive woman with broad cultural interests. In the sophisticated atmosphere of Berlin, the capital city, she had grown up exposed from early youth to the theater, to books and to witty conversation. Her ancestors were highly regarded scholars and civil servants. But whatever their accomplishments, they were only middle-class commoners, for whom marriage into a noble family meant an immense gain of status. This explains the unlikely union which was concluded when she was seventeen and the groom thirty-five.

Wilhelmine found Pomeranian country life extremely uninspiring. She was not about to bury herself behind the thick walls of the Kniephof no matter how deeply the peasant bowed when she rode by. Usually the Prussian male ruled his family with an iron hand, but Ferdinand was no match for the determined mind of his young spouse. When Otto was seven years old, he had to say good-bye to the deferential villagers, to pony rides in the forest and games around the haystacks in the fields.

At his mother's insistence, they all headed for Berlin, where Wilhelmine proceeded to embrace the life of high society. A fashionable apartment on Opera Square was rented, and Frau von Bismarck saw to it that it was lavishly furnished with Persian carpets and huge oil canvases framed in heavy gold. She spent far too much money, yet she was never satisfied. Looking around the rooms she complained, "This is all so ordinary and cheap. How can we entertain here the people who really matter?"

Her husband just shook his head in helpless resignation. To provide the means for all these extravagances, he shuttled back and forth between the capital and his estates trying to make the labor of his peasants finance the costly Berlin establishment. But it did not work out. The debts accumulated since he was too easygoing to worry much about them.

Wilhelmine was not devoid of motherly feelings, but her love had a hard and cutting edge. The nervous, overwrought woman was passionately ambitious for her sons. Especially in Otto she sensed an unusual talent which needed to be developed. Her mind was all made up that he was to follow in her own father's footsteps, for Ludwig Mencken had been a distinguished member of the higher Prussian bureaucracy. Otto seemed to be cut out for a diplomatic career, and with her social connections she hoped to make it possible. Connections and titles were the main prerequisites for such positions. Once Otto was within the ranks of the foreign service, it would be up to him to work himself up the ladder of promotion. Though he was only of the lower nobility, he could, with some luck, even end up as an ambassador to some smaller capital, such as Berne or The Hague.

Clever and well informed, Frau von Bismarck sensed the tremendous opportunities in the field of diplomacy. Exciting things were about to happen. The air seemed to vibrate with the forebodings of change. Such times, she felt, always offer unique opportunities to men of courage who are close to the seats of power.

Europe was not just one of several continents; it was the hub of the world. Europeans considered the remainder of the globe a backward no-man's-land waiting to be conquered. With the help of steam and some amazing new inventions, English cities were turning into grimy machine shops, but the continent was still mostly populated by peasants plowing behind their horses or oxen. They paid scant attention to the warring armies moving hither and yonder and once in a while giving battle in some loamy fields. Royal courts vied with each other in luxury and ostentation, and the towns were controlled by proud merchant families. Poets and musicians lived in a romantic dreamworld which they found much more attractive than the drab realities around them.

Four heavily armed nation states dominated the international scene. England, Russia and Austria had just emerged victoriously from the Napoleonic wars and had collected rich spoils. Smaller states were not of much account, and the United States of America had yet to assume its seat in the concert of great nations. On the other hand, France, though shorn of her recent conquests, had again joined the first league in the international competition for power.

In this political world series, two teams destined to play major roles were still missing. Italy and Germany were absent for the simple reason that they did not exist. But in both areas powerful movements were afoot to correct this deficiency. On Italian soil, fiery poets and romantic privateers were already clamoring loudly for national unification.

Germany had, for centuries, been no more than a geographic name, a label for a crazy quilt of independent states. They came in every size and shape, and they were all fiercely jealous of one another, continuously embroiled in bloody infighting. Of those three hundred or so political entities, Austria was the most powerful. Her rulers, the Habsburgs, were nominally the emperors of all Germans. But this was only an empty title which lingered on through the centuries till Napoleon officially condemned it to a long-overdue death.

The Habsburgs ruled over a strange assortment of subjects. Only one fifth of the thirty million Austrians spoke German. The remainder of their lands, which the Habsburgs seemed to collect as individuals collect stamps, were inhabited by Slavs, Hungarians, Italians and others. The emperors in Vienna were not choosy. But when they continued to pose as the natural leaders of all Germans, their royal colleagues on the various German thrones became suspicious. They did not want to see their lands swallowed up by the insatiable Habsburgs. Nor did the Austrian rulers sound very convincing as the spokesmen for a unified Germany since they had so many non-German subjects.

Still the clamor for German unification grew louder. A strong nationalistic sentiment pervaded the younger generation. "Why can't we Germans be strong like other nations?" asked many. They sang of Germany's beauty and of its glorious past. Romantic idealists proclaimed the brotherhood of all Germans from the Rhine to the Oder.

The princes of Europe cared little about such popular feelings. While Napoleon was bemoaning his fate in exile, they and their ministers haggled over boundaries at the Congress of Vienna. Cities and provinces were traded back and forth like so many pieces of real estate.

The representatives of Prussia turned out to be the most skillful land traders in the business. When the long drawn-out Congress finally came to an end, they emerged with the choicest bargains. The Prussian land gains were all at the expense of the other German states, whose number had been reduced to thirty-nine. With a population of over ten million, Prussia was now the number one contender for the leading role in the process of unification. The great powers of Europe also began to look at her with a new respect.

It had not always been so. At first the house of Hohenzollern ruled only over the small duchy of Brandenburg. By brutal force, by threats and bribes, it gradually expanded its holdings till the black-and-white Prussian flag flew over large patches of Northern Germany from Poland to France. At one point along this road to power, the Hohenzollern rulers adopted the title of King. This sounded much more grandiose than Prince Elector, which had been their earlier designation.

In the eighteenth century, King Frederick the Great spread Prussia's fame for the first time beyond the confines of the German world. He was a philosopher and a friend of the common people. But this did not impress the crowned heads of Europe as much as the fact that he created the most efficient fighting force on the continent. It covered itself with glory by soundly defeating the Austrian armies.

Prussia was on the march, and she marched with the high jackboots of her soldiers. Frederick the Great and later Hohenzollerns lavished overwhelming doses of money and attention on the army. Prussia became the strongpoint of modern militarism, a state of mind which considers soldiering the most desirable human activity. A uniform with shiny buttons, snapping to attention, bellowing orders and, above all, unquestioning obedience—those became the characteristics of a country which, in a way, was really an oversized army barracks.

Napoleon's victories had come as quite a shock to these militarists, especially to the Junker class. But when Otto's family moved to Berlin, the cocky Prussian spirit was beginning to assert itself again. The trauma of defeat had worn off. While the militarists were talking again of conquests to make Prussia even more powerful, the nationalists wanted Prussia to submerge in a united Germany. These two movements were headed for a collision.

A greater Prussia or a unified German nation—these were the alternatives. And if a German nation should arise, who would unify it? Only two serious candidates with enough power and ambition were in the running: the Habsburgs with their ancient claim to leadership and the latecomers in Berlin with their crack army. These were the questions which would confront Otto if he were to submit to his mother's guidance.

For a future diplomat Berlin was just the right place in which to grow up. It was a city which exuded efficiency. Officers in tightly corsetted uniforms and bureaucrats in frockcoats and uncomfortably high collars crowded the intersection of Friedrichstrasse and Unter den Linden (Under the Linden Trees), the two major thoroughfares. A rapidly thickening ring of bleak tenements sprawled around a core of stern government buildings and fashionable residences over which towered magnificently the royal palace.

But at the age of seven, Otto felt uncomfortable and lonely in these new surroundings. His father was a nonentity who did not belong here. Mother, on the other hand, was in her element, but she hardly had any time for her children. She was able to wheedle invitations to the most exclusive gatherings. Her proudest accomplishment was that she had managed to be introduced to King Frederick William III himself.

Occasionally a court messenger knocked at the door of the apartment on Opera Square, and announced: "The young Royal Highnesses wish to play with your sons, Frau von Bismarck." Then Otto and Bernhard, dressed in their finest, rode in the royal carriage behind a liveried coachman to spend a few hours with the King's two sons. They ran races through the immense palace gardens or sailed model ships on the marble-fringed pools. Otto did not like these visits, for he had been instructed beforehand that one must never argue with the young princes, and it was best to let them win at the races. It was very hard for him to keep from demonstrating to the boys that they were not very bright.

Certinly all this was no substitute for a mother's tenderness. Otto was overawed by her beauty and by the grandiose manners she displayed. In his famous autobiography he described her as she appeared to him before leaving for some gala evening at a cabinet minister's residence: "She wore long gloves and a dress with a narrow waist, a big hairdo with many curls and a big ostrich feather in her hair."

He also wrote of the many receptions and dinners at his home when the rooms were crowded with men in uniform twirling their oiled mustaches, bowing to the ladies from the waist and gallantly kissing their gloved hands. He watched the glittering spectacle from a corner, unnoticed, till a chambermaid would come and lead him away. In the kitchen she stuffed him with caviar and sweets prepared for the banquet table. They were choice tidbits, but his little stomach had trouble digesting them. Then she packed him off to his room. Mother was far too busy for a bedtime story or a good-night kiss.

"My mother liked to go out and mingle with high society, and she didn't pay much attention to us." Written decades later, these words still reflect the resentment of a little boy. He could barely conceal his aversion to the woman who failed him, just when, transplanted into a strange environment, he needed her most.

Yet the two were very much alike. Otto seemed to have inherited much of his mother's talent and temper. Both possessed keen minds and a ready wit which could sparkle and also sear.

He did not feel very close to his brother, a slow-going youth with little drive or ambition. Only when a sister arrived on the scene did

Otto find somebody to love. To Malvine, who was twelve years younger, he remained attached throughout her life with unusually tender ties.

Repelled by his mother's coldness, he voiced lifelong deep affection for a father from whom he seemed to have inherited nothing, except stature and physical strength. But the aging squire gave what Otto needed most: kindness. He never scolded and he never chided his sons for failing to live up to anybody's expectations. Whatever they achieved was sufficient for him. He put up with his wife's extravagances without any protest, except for some occasional good-humored joshing. Wilhelmine dabbled in spiritualism and occultism, fads which were fashionable in her circles. She maintained that she had powers of clairvoyance and could discern things which normally remained hidden. Her husband wanted to know, "If you possess second sight, how come you didn't foresee the fall of the wool prices on the exchange? I could have saved myself a lot of money."

Money and love—despite the glittering outward appearance, these two commodities were in short supply at the Bismarck residence.

✠ 2 ✠

MAD JUNKER

"VON BISMARCK," BARKED THE TEACHER. HE SPAT OUT THE "VON" with a nasty sneer. Otto shot up from the battered schoolbench which he shared with two other pupils. "Yes, Herr Teacher."

He stood erect, eyes focused on the schoolmaster as had been drilled into the boys.

"You were late again for morning gymnastics in the yard. It is the third time this term. This is not your country estate, and we are not peasants who jump at your command. Here you obey the rules. As a punishment you will copy ten pages from the reader this afternoon. Sit down."

"Yes, Herr Teacher. I am sorry, Herr Teacher."

He fought back the tears. Under no circumstances would he have cried before these hostile people. His noble birth made him an outcast in the eyes of teachers and other pupils. Yet he could not claim to have been unjustly punished. He had indeed broken the rule. Each morning at the crack of dawn, when the headmaster banged at the dormitory door with the pommel of a saber, he had a terrible time getting up.

In the afternoons there were more physical exercises in the yard, and afterward they played games. Even then he was an outsider.

"Hey, *Von,*" shouted a boy. "You're bleeding from a scratch on your arm. It's red. I thought you noble guys had blue blood."

"Just plain ordinary red blood like the rest of us," echoed another, accompanied by the loud guffaws of his friends.

What could Otto do? Fight them all? Impossible. He just pretended not to have heard and turned away for a solitary jog around the yard.

So went the days at the *Plamannsche Anstalt,* a boys' boarding school on the outskirts of Berlin. It was a progressive private institution with much stress on physical toughness. The food was coarse, the blankets were thin, but discipline was as harsh as in any Prussian school.

Most children of the aristocracy received their elementary education through private tutors at home, but Frau von Bismarck insisted on having Otto out of the house by the time he reached grade school age.

At the *Plamannsche Anstalt,* faculty and fellow students were all of the middle class, and most teachers had strongly liberal convictions. Liberalism was the young moving force among the intellectuals all over Europe. It stood for freedom of personal expression and opposed political and religious tyranny. Liberals demanded some form of constitutional government, which was then still denied the citizens of most countries. They emphatically condemned the unrestrained powers of princes and the undeserved privileges of a hereditary noble class.

On the other hand, most aristocrats were staunchly conservative. They wanted no change from the present status which gave them such pleasant advantages. Any reform would be at their expense.

Otto was caught in the growing antagonism between liberals and conservatives. Stung by the barbed remarks of his teachers and the coarse pranks of his fellow pupils, he learned to hate the word "liberal" long before he quite understood what it meant. He desperately missed his home, and he yearned for the security he had felt in the peaceful meadows of the family estate. "When I saw from the window a team of oxen pull a plow," he wrote as an adult, "I had to cry pining for the Kniephof."

The situation was not much better when, at the age of twelve, he transferred to the *gymnasium,* the academic high school which was the gateway to all occupations above the level of manual labor. Most professors there were also committed to liberal ideas and therefore admired Voltaire and John Locke, whose words had inflamed the minds of revolutionaries in America and in France.

Despite the rough treatment he received, Otto could not help being influenced by the intensive liberal exposure at the *gymnasium.* His writings contain the confession: "I left the school at Eastertime of the year 1832 as a pantheist and with the conviction that the republican form of government was the most reasonable one."

Pantheism does not recognize the existence of a personal God; therefore it has no place for prayer or any other form of worship. Otto never went to church, and neither did his free-thinking mother. His attitude of supreme indifference toward religion stayed with him for many years, but the republican notions he quickly got out of his system. They conflicted too obviously with the strongly rooted Junker virtue of submission to authority. Everybody has a master above him to whom he owes unquestioning obedience, and the supreme master is the one who directs the machinery of the state.

As he studied history, he came to despise the heroes who owed their fame to rebellion against authority. His dislike extended to Brutus, who helped slay Julius Caesar, and even to the legendary William Tell, whose arrow had dispatched the oppressor of his Swiss homeland.

Otto's record as a pupil was no more than average. He could easily have been at the top of the class, had he applied himself and had he not constantly argued with his professors, who often complained about his rebellious nature. While denying his fellowmen the right to protest, he found himself unable to submit to the will of others. Still he passed the very exacting battery of final exams, the *abitur,* and graduated fifteenth in a class of eighteen.

The next indispensable way station for a young man of good family, especially for a budding diplomat, was the university. Otto enrolled at Göttingen in the German state of Hanover. German universities were just coming into their own. In the past they had remained woefully behind the institutions of higher learning in England and France. Now some were making great strides in such fields as philosophy, history and the natural sciences.

The University of Göttingen provided an excellent climate for scholarship, but Otto von Bismarck did not avail himself of the opportunities. In fact, he hardly spent any time inside the academic halls, except when he was called before the provost who handled disciplinary matters, and that happened quite frequently. For three consecutive terms he enrolled in the courses of a particularly famed professor, but he attended his lectures only twice during the whole time.

What else then does a seventeen-year-old youth do in a little university town? Bismarck had no trouble filling the days. There existed a tradition of revelry and mayhem with which first-year students celebrated their new freedom after the long confinement in the lower schools.

The evening hours were passed in the beer gardens and wine cellars without which no German university town could exist. The student corps which Otto had joined met regularly in one such place. The members wore their flat caps and breast ribbons, all in the corps colors. Some brought their foils and sabers to the meetings; others substituted heavy walking canes.

Even in the act of carousing there had to be discipline. They broke into their corps songs at the command of the president. In between songs, he shouted, *"Achtung*—Great Salamander." Hastily they filled the two-quart beer steins. Then came the command, *"Eins— zwei—drei*—drink up." With precise arm movements they all raised their goblets to their lips and drained them in one gigantic swig. Anybody who failed was penalized by having to consume extra steins.

Those young men appreciated Otto's company. They were his own kind. Nobody mentioned liberalism, except as a curse word. It was good to be counted among the privileged rather than to be the underdog. "I am a Junker," he exclaimed, "and I mean to have the advantages of that position."

Yet even as a playboy-student he did not fit the mold. He gladly caroused with his noble companions, but despised their dull minds. Many a night, after the others had stumbled to their quarters, he wandered alone down to the Leine River, stripped off his clothes and swam long and without any sound in the soft moonlit water, abandoning himself to melancholy brooding.

The raucous noise of the tavern left him depressed and nauseated. Where did he really belong? What was his purpose? He felt contempt for his drinking companions and even more contempt for himself. So he swam on, seeking relief in physical exhaustion. Only when the dawn colored water and sky a dark purple did he feel that all his huge supply of energy had been expended, and he returned to town.

He slept late into the morning. There was nobody to punish him now for being late at exercises. Then he walked the streets with the sole purpose of arousing attention. He received it in generous quantities. His reddish hair hung down to his neck. Above one red-veined eye the brow was shaved off. A huge fiery scar extended from the nose to the right ear. He wore a velvet coat without collar or buttons, enormous wide trousers and high boots with iron heels. At every step a pair of spurs emitted a loud clanging. But this was not enough. A huge saber was strapped to his waist, and a fierce-looking yellow dog trotted by his side.

This apparition caused incredulous stares. Here and there one could hear laughter. If it reached the ear of the young eccentric, he turned and stepped up to the culprit. Those who were not corps students hurriedly withdrew from a confrontation with the towering figure. But men of Otto's own kind could hardly do that.

"Were you laughing at me, *Herr Kollege?*" The question was asked in a deliberately courteous tone. Since there was no denying that this had indeed been the case, the challenger continued, "I demand satisfaction. You have the choice of saber or foil. My seconds will see you shortly and make arrangements for tomorrow morning. Good day, sir."

Formal bows on both sides. The interview was over. Master and dog moved on. Perhaps the same walk might yield a second duel for the same day. Bismarck was insatiable when it came to picking formal fights. In one summer he fought the incredible number of thirty-two such duels, strange leftovers from the days of knights in armor. One of the encounters had caused the scar which adorned Otto's face. Far from bewailing this disfigurement, he cherished it as a visible testimony to his manliness.

For a duel he did not mind getting up at an early hour. In a large attic room above a tavern, the two combatants met accompanied by their seconds and a doctor. Stripped to the waist, they greeted each other ceremoniously with lowered foils. Then they began to slash away. It was a dangerous game which not rarely ended in permanent injury, sometimes in death. Bismarck's superb skill and top physical conditioning made him the terror of the *fechtboden* (fencing hall). As his opponent began letting blood in large quantities, the medic stepped in to halt the fight. The adversaries bowed and shook hands. The demands of the academic honor code had been met.

Despite all those capers, Bismarck managed to further his education, but mostly outside the university walls. He read copious material of his own choice, especially when he was abed sick. This happened rather frequently despite his splendid physique. His illnesses were mostly caused by overindulging. At one occasion he astounded his dinner companions by consuming one hundred and fifty oysters.

His sensitive mind demanded as large quantities of nourishment as did his huge body. He absorbed the works of the philosopher Spinoza and tried, not too successfully, to plow unaided through the obtuse volumes of Hegel. Since he commanded both the French and the English languages with ease, his choice of reading material was considerable. English authors were his favorites. He enjoyed Walter Scott and Lord Byron and became an admirer of Shakespeare's works. This man who was to be hailed as the very essence of everything German remained attracted to British ways all his life. Even the

British political system found his warm approval, though he did not consider it applicable to his own fatherland.

His considerable linguistic talent enabled him to read ancient Greek and Roman authors in the original. Later in life, he liked to adorn his conversation and his speeches with classical quotations. This was done to impress the listeners rather than to transmit classical thought. He had neither the temperament nor the inclination to engage in philosophical speculation or in quiet scholarly searching.

Three careers were open to the scion of Junker blood: civil service, the army and the management of his own land. Bismarck was to try them all in this order, and abandon all three with disgust.

A law degree was the essential entrance ticket to the ranks of the state bureaucracy. To earn one as quickly as possible, Otto transferred to the University of Berlin. It was of a more recent date than most German universities, but already housed a galaxy of famous scholars. Until recently the lectures of the philosopher Georg Friedrich Hegel had been the main attraction there, and even after his death, professors did little more than expound the involved speculations of Hegelianism.

Certainly there was enough to stimulate a highly gifted intellect. But Bismarck was not interested. Only toward the end of his three terms in Berlin did he settle down, not to wrestle with ideas, but to cram night and day. Private "cramming instructors" made a precarious living drilling such absentee students as Otto for their final examinations. His outrageously sharp mind overcame in a few weeks the neglect of several years, and he passed easily.

Armed with his law diploma, he knocked at the formidable doors of the state establishment to claim his reward. Prussia had developed an effective system of public administration which was the envy of other countries. Yet it was mechanical and it stymied personal initiative. Mountains of records were stacked up in dusty offices, not only in Berlin but in all the provincial and district branches. The lower echelons of the civil service pedantically followed myriads of regulations while their superiors made up new ones, strangulating the simplest matters in tight webs of red tape. By keeping their thoughts to themselves and by cultivating the right connections, the young men slowly moved up the ladder of advancement. Their fond hope was that someday they might hear themselves addressed as *Herr Geheimrat* (Mr. Privy Councilor). With this coveted title they would reach the pinnacle of their careers.

Dutifully, but without enthusiasm, Bismarck started at the bottom as an *auscultator,* a kind of secretary to a judge. His job was to keep records of court proceedings. After a year of such humdrum work and a further examination, he stepped up to the level of *referendar,* a trial judge in minor cases.

He was sent to the city of Aachen. In the cold, badly ventilated government building he listlessly questioned small-time pilferers and drunks. A bachelor himself, he handled divorce cases with little excitement. Soon he developed a strong aversion to his work and to Prussian officialdom in general, which he described as "dried out by the dust of reports, weak in breast and bowels from endless sitting."

Only after office hours did life become more enticing. Aachen, located near the French and Belgian borders, was part of the Rhineland which had only recently been acquired by Prussia. Its social life was cosmopolitan; compared to it Berlin was a provincial backwater. The famous sulphur springs made the city a thermal resort for the wealthy and their minions. Elegant ladies dressed in the latest Paris fashions promenaded under the ornate colonades. Except for taking the waters at regulated hours, they had nothing to do; so they filled the days and nights with entertainment and flirtation.

The tall Junker who now sported reddish-brown whiskers was in his element. He patronized the most expensive tailors and visited the finest restaurants. The meagerness of his salary was no obstacle, since his name and position opened him unlimited credit—at twelve percent interest.

Gone were the crude manners and the ridiculous garb of the Göttingen days. With his charm and quick wit he became the life of many a party. Especially the British ladies found him irresistible. His command of foreign languages was now an invaluable asset.

When the financial situation became hopeless, he tried to erase the deficit at the gaming tables. Predictably he lost huge amounts. Even his father, who had never scolded him or urged him on to higher accomplishments, finally lost his patience. He categorically refused to make good Otto's debts. This was disconcerting news coming on top of the eternally reproachful letters from his mother. Frau von Bismarck was an unhappy woman frustrated in her hopes for the brilliant son's future and now prematurely wasting away with the torments of incurable cancer.

Yet all this did not worry the *Herr Referendar*. He was amusing himself with Laura Russell, the daughter of an English duke. But the social distance between a young duchess and a mere Junker with nothing to his name but a very humble position and very substantial debts was too wide for a lasting bond. Soon he consoled himself with other romantic adventures. For a time he squired blonde, willowy Isabelle Loraine, another tender flower of British womanhood. With humbler ancestry—she was the daughter of a preacher—she was more within reach.

Otto so completely lost his head over the attractive lady that he forgot his duties. Taking a two-week leave from his work, he followed his beloved on a tour of many European tourist spots. Without bothering with formalities, he stayed away from his desk for six months. In his letters to friends and relatives, engagement and marriage were mentioned, but in the end, cool, calculating Isabelle threw him over in favor of a fifty-one-year-old one-armed horsebreeder with a fat bank account. They were married two months after she broke with the Prussian.

It was a rude awakening. Otto never returned to Aachen. It went against his whole nature to come crawling to his superiors with a prayer for forgiveness, and he loathed his job anyhow. Only his family status and certain connections in high places prevented his name from being blacklisted by all government agencies. With surprising leniency the authorities offered him a second chance. He was sent to Potsdam, sixteen miles from Berlin. Much governmental activity was still concentrated in this former residence of the Hohenzollern rulers.

But Bismarck was not ready to mend his ways. Repeating his Aachen performance, he absented himself after three months without so much as saying good-bye. From all appearances this was the end of his connection with Prussian officialdom. Somewhat prophetically his superior at Potsdam made the following entry in his records: "If Herr von Bismarck can succeed in overcoming his personal laziness, then he will be capable of filling the highest offices in the state."

What next? Now it was not up to him to decide. Having ceased to be a civilian servant of the state, he was automatically liable for compulsory military service. The pain was eased by the prerogative of his class. The *von* in front of his name earned him immediately a lieutenant's insignia.

Young Bismarck looked just like the person who would have taken to army life with relish. Prussian officers strutted through the streets like little gods, contemptuously receiving as their due the salutes of the lesser ranks. Everywhere they claimed and received special privileges. Yet Otto abhorred the notion of military life and pleaded all sorts of imaginary ailments, such as muscular weakness in one arm, to stay out of uniform. But it was to no avail.

Despite his tall frame and upright carriage, the Pomeranian Junker proved to be no great asset to the Prussian officers' corps. Almost as soon as he had joined a regiment of the royal guards, he got into hot water with the commander. The rigid discipline for which the Prussian forces were famous was not for him. He had no difficulty ordering others around, but he could not stand being on the receiving end. He barely lived through the minimum time of compulsory service without being court-martialed. At the first possible moment he asked for his release.

At the age of twenty-four Bismarck was a failure in two vocations without feeling any regret. Officers and civil servants, he said, had to be members of an orchestra and submit to the conductor's baton. "But I will play music the way I like it, or not at all." Those were proud words coming from the lips of an unemployed university graduate.

In the meantime his mother, only fifty years old, had died. Her last years had been a tragic physical and mental ordeal. She had failed in seeing her own ambitions fulfilled in her son. When asked what he wanted to do now, Otto was quite definite, "I am going to be a country gentleman. I belong in the clean air, in the green forests and on the good black soil. This is the life I crave. Also I can make more money on the land and I certainly need it."

He could not have been more wrong. It took him eight miserable years to find out. Like his mother, he was not cut out to stagnate as an exile from the glitter and the excitement of the city.

But for the present he was determined to follow in the footsteps, of his father, who was now in his seventies. The family finances were catastrophic. Due to poor management, the land holdings were run down and in danger of being lost. In a last effort to keep them in the family, old Bismark concentrated on the Schönhausen estate while his sons divided among themselves what was left. Otto became the master of the Kniephof where he had spent a few happy years of his childhood.

The outdoor life was indeed enjoyable. Speeding on big Kaleb, his favorite horse, across the meadows gave Otto a never ending thrill. Gladly he rose before dawn to stalk game through the dripping forest. It was soothing to the nerves to glide in a boat along the slow river in search of wild ducks.

Bravely he attempted to be a competent agricultural manager, and he met with undeniable success. Now he was the one to give orders, and he did so wisely and effectively. His mind easily absorbed new knowledge in the fields of scientific farming, chemistry and marketing. Big bundles of books and pamphlets arrived at the Kniephof for the perusal of the master.

He treated his peasants well. Not that he ever allowed any familiarity, but as long as they approached him with the right amount of humility, he was willing to be their patriarchal protector. It worked since everybody seemed to know and keep his place.

But could all this satisfy a mind of Bismarck's capacity? The harder he tried, the more painful became the feeling of utter frustration.

There he sat in his shabby library with the damask tapestries hanging in tatters from the walls. The wind howled through the fireplace chimney, endlessly repeating its desolate tune of loneliness. The shelves were buckling under fresh loads of books which arrived almost daily in the mail. Bismarck got a great deal of good reading done in those years: history, geography and lots of English novels. He learned more at the Kniephof than he ever had at the university. But it was not enough. He could never be happy as a scholarly recluse. Vaguely he talked of seeking his fortune in remote lands, perhaps in Egypt or in India. What he really needed was people, partners for stimulating conversation, willing human material on whom he could try the ideas gleaned from his books. Where were they to be found? Certainly not at or near the Kniephof.

Occasionally he escaped the oppressive dullness of his surroundings by traveling to England or to the fashionable North Sea resorts. Hungrily he plunged into the titillating social whirl only to find his little world even more depressing upon his return.

With the peasants one could only talk about seeds and manure. And for his noble neighbors Bismarck had nothing but contempt. Those narrow-minded squires were good as drinking and hunting companions. That was all. Nobody could castigate them with bitterer scorn than their fellow Junker did in his letters, especially those addressed to his sister Malvine. She had moved with him to the Kniephof when she was thirteen years old. But four years later, she left as a young bride. So ended the only warm relationship Otto had found. From then on he poured his woes into a constant flow of letters to her which sound almost like a lover's messages to his beloved. We find him addressing his sister as "my angel" and "my adored one" and concluding with "Farewell for now, my love. Wholly your own, Otto."

Out of sheer boredom he reverted to the juvenile escapades of his Göttingen days. Recklessly he galloped on Kaleb through the hamlets. Peasants and even his neighbors took to hiding their daughters when they saw him approaching. On nightly drunken forays, he liked to awaken his acquaintances with wild pistol shots through windows which sent the plaster trickling from the ceiling over the sleepers. His pent-up energy seemed to find release only in immoderate indulgence and in acts of destruction. The tenants nicknamed him the Mad Junker, and he did everything to live up to the name.

To a friend he remarked, "You know, either I shall become the biggest scoundrel or the greatest man in Prussia." At the moment the second alternative seemed very remote.

✠ 3 ✠

FIGHTING JUNKER

"You and you and you, make haste with those wheelbar-
rows. Bring more sand and pile it up over there where the water is
seeping through."

"Yes, Herr Dike Captain. Let's hope the dike holds."

"Hurry, men, The ice jam may break any moment. If you move
fast, we can still win this battle."

It was past midnight. Smoky pine torches illuminated the scene.
Bismarck stood knee-deep in the numbing cold water of the Elbe
River. The water oozed over the rims of his high boots into the
soggy clothing, yet he was exuberant. He was fighting the elements
and he was directing men.

After his father's death in 1845, he had moved to Schönhausen,
the place of his birth. The other family holdings had been leased
out. Tired of solitary reading and of the endless carousing with
thick-headed neighbors, he finally found an outlet for his surging
vitality. The Elbe flowed only one mile from the estate. Every year
it went on a rampage, killing livestock and eroding the soil of valuable croplands. For ages the squires whose land lay along the river
banks had elected one of their own to be the dike captain. His task
was to direct the peasants in maintaining the levees. At the dangerous moment in early spring, when the ice threatened to break, he
was to lead them in the fight against the destructive waters.

Bismarck seized upon this chance for leadership. But to obtain such a rather modest position he first had to dislodge the incumbent. Without hesitation he accomplished this by personally complaining to all the neighbors that the present captain was too often absent from the job. He also let it slip into the conversation that since his estate lay so close to the danger points, he could render better service than all possible candidates. With such persistence and a remarkable lack of modesty, he convinced them that he was the man for the job.

And he proved that the boast was justified. Almost visibly he grew in stature. Everybody in sight lent a willing hand, as if mesmerized by the tall figure rising from the swirling water. The dike held.

Finally Bismarck was in his element. After many wasted years the realization had come: his role in life was to wield power, to force his will upon others. But nobody was offering him such opportunities; he had to go after them, he had to fight for the right to lead. Only by ruthlessly pushing obstacles out of his way could he get where he wanted to go.

The dike job was only a training exercise. He knew now where he really belonged. Abandoning all other interests, including the care of his farms, he threw himself into the whirlpool of politics. He was still unknown to the world, one of many hundred Prussian Junkers sitting on their ancestral lands, far away from the capitals where the destinies of states were hammered out.

Bismarck's first political position was as a member of the Pomeranian provincial Diet. Again he had to employ cunning and rough tactics to obtain the seat. His opportunity came when a regular member became ill and a replacement was needed. At the next election the man was ready to run again, but Bismarck, unwilling to relinquish the slender toehold on public life, pressured all his noble friends to persuade his predecessor that his health was still too delicate for the rigors of politics. The Junker from Schönhausen was determined and he succeeded.

Never one to be plagued by excessive modesty, he immediately stepped into the limelight. He spoke up on any subject, though the issues before this legislative body of a largely rural province were mostly of a rather lightweight nature. Vehemently and eloquently he argued, for example, that a certain wretched almshouse in a little town had used up too much tallow during the past year.

A wider battlefield opened up when Bismarck was sent to represent the provincial body in the United Diet of Prussia which met in Berlin. It was a curious relic of bygone centuries, constituting anything but a true representation of the Prussian people. On the throne sat Frederick William IV, the older of the two Hohenzollern brothers whom Otto had known in his boyhood days. He meant well, but he was weak and unstable. His recurring moods of depression signaled already the approach of severe mental illness which would eventually put an end to his reign.

Frederick William desperately wanted to be loved by all his subjects. Any criticism was taken as a personal insult, an expression of ingratitude. Wasn't he "King by the grace of God"? He took this antiquated formula quite literally. People had no rights except those he in his fatherly benevolence decided to bestow upon them.

It was kindhearted of him, he reasoned, to allow his subjects a diet at all. There the delegates could deliberate to their heart's content, but never override the sovereign's will. It was, as some observers called it, just a "debating society."

The Diet was a medieval institution dusted off by a King who was himself a throwback to the Middle Ages. He wanted society to remain, as of old, divided into rigid social classes, all enveloped in the incense of a strongly authoritarian type of Christianity. The delegates to the United Diet represented not the population at large, but their own class, such as the nobility, the city dwellers and the peasantry. This and the fact that voting rights depended on the ownership of property gave the aristocracy an overwhelming advantage.

The King was a romantic as were many writers and artists of the time who liked to glorify the past. But whereas the poets could only sing and dream, the monarch was in a position to upset things thoroughly with his outdated notions. Prussia was then a police state where schools and universities were under strict surveillance and where an extremely narrow-minded censorship shackled the press and the platform. Such a system might work well for a time, provided there was firm and understanding guidance from the top. This was not the case.

Though the Diet was heavily weighted toward the conservative viewpoint, the voices of liberalism came through loud and strong. The middle class had sent some of its best minds to the assembly, among them renowned scholars and persuasive orators. Even in the ranks of the nobility could be found some enlightened individuals who championed a mild dose of democracy because they wanted Prussia to be a modern and progressive state.

Bismarck was in his element. "I hear the trumpet," he wrote in a letter. "I must join the battle. I have a natural craving for combat." This was a more significant battlefield than the dueling chamber in Göttingen. On the fourth day of the session he already stood at the speaker's rostrum.

It was not the most polished speech the delegates had ever heard. With surprise they noted the contrast between the imposing figure of the freshman member and his squeaky high-pitched voice. He stuttered and stumbled over his own words. The more excited he became, the worse it got. Yet they were soon sitting at the edge of their chairs. Never before had they witnessed such an exhibition of arrogance and vilification.

A previous speaker had recalled a promise made by the present King's father. In the darkest days of French occupation, Frederick William III had pledged to grant a constitution and to give guarantees of personal freedom. After the enemy had been expelled, the pledge was conveniently forgotten. The mild reproach made by a distinguished veteran of the Napoleonic wars gave Bismarck his opening. Brutally disregarding all the respect due an older colleague, he shrieked, "The defense of the fatherland requires no reward. To ask for one is an insult to Prussian honor. It shows lack of patriotic feeling—"

The chamber was in uproar. Shouts of outrage, trampling feet and banging fists drowned out the presiding officer's plea for order. Bismarck's reaction to all this pandemonium was studied contempt.

He turned his back to the assembly, pulled a newspaper from his pocket and began to read, waiting for the noise to subside.

This was his debut as a political fighter. In it he deployed the whole arsenal of weapons which he was determined to use. In the future he would only hone them to greater efficiency, give them an even finer cutting edge. With his special brand of merciless sarcasm, he not only argued issues but attacked the loyalty, the intelligence, even the honesty of everybody who incurred his disfavor. Even outside the formal sessions, he did not grant his opponents the courtesies common among civilized people. Nor did he spare his own partisans, whom he tactlessly gave to understand that they were not his equals in intelligence.

It did not take long till Bismarck had the dubious distinction of being the most-hated member of the Diet. From the chamber this reputation was carried into the streets. On his walks he was met with jeers and catcalls. Occasionally he had to duck stones and other missiles aimed at his head. But far from being cowed, the delegate from Schönhausen actually thrived on all this hostility. It gave him just the right incentive to fight on with even more savage thrusts.

He was at his best when he fought *against* rather than *for* something. But gradually, as he attacked and parried, he adopted a political viewpoint of his own. It was not particularly original, nor was it permanent. Bismarck was essentially a pragmatist. For him live action always came before principle. But in the United Diet he was tagged as the spokesman of the ultraconservative wing. His name became a synonym for the most reactionary tendencies.

In speech after speech he castigated any attempt to limit the power of the king or the inherited privileges of the landed gentry. For him democracy was an evil word denoting anarchy and mob rule. Revolutions were the work of the devil no matter what the cause. The authorities were not only justified but duty-bound to repress them with bullets and prison bars. Only men with breeding—meaning possessors of hereditary titles—were capable of holding responsible positions.

While he made ample use of his own right to speak out, he was determined to deny it to those holding opposing views. "We must not suffer any opposition," he thundered. "We must stand united under our beloved ruler."

His pragmatism led him to voice contradictory views. He would not completely do away with parliamentary institutions. There was some value in mild criticism even of the royal person, he felt, "in order to guard the monarch against the danger that women, courtiers, overambitious servants and dreamers put blinders on him."

On social questions he was unbending and also rather uninformed. He just did not realize that the world was changing. The most antiquated feudal privileges of which even his fellow aristocrats were ashamed found in him a champion. He fought a losing battle against any changes in the unrestricted hunting rights of the landlord on his land. While the squire could, at will, trample into dust the peasant's crop, the poor devil was forbidden to shoot the rabbits which were devouring his food for the next winter. "The expropriation of such well-earned rights against the will of the owners," Bismarck argued, "would lead to communism."

As a Junker from the rural hinterlands, he was strongly prejudiced against the cities which, as he claimed, the middle class was turning into hotbeds of rebellion. His understanding of urban problems remained deficient throughout his life. Therefore it is hardly surprising that he chimed into the frequent reactionary outcries against the Jews, who lived mainly in the towns. To the liberals who stood for equal rights of all citizens regardless of religion, he said, "I am bored with this sentimental humanitarian drivel."

The Diet did not give Bismarck sufficient opportunities to work out his political energies, and so he branched out into journalism and became one of the chief contributors to the *Kreuzzeitung* (*Cross Journal*), the mouthpiece of the farthest right. Besides, he engaged in endless behind-the-scene plotting and intrigue. Those activities he eventually perfected to unequaled heights of mastery.

His old connections with the royal court came in handy. He was invited to receptions and to pleasure cruises on the nearby lakes and rivers. Particularly important was the acquaintance with the King's younger brother William, whose official title was "Prince of Prussia," as distinguished from the King of Prussia. Since the monarch had no children, William was the rightful heir to the throne.

One would have expected the King to be extremely pleased with Bismarck's philosophy. Perhaps he was, but he found it wise not to show the Junker any favors in public. Knowing how widely this man was loathed, he preferred to keep him at a distance. Bismarck himself observed:

> At the court festivities which took place during the session of the United Diet, I was avoided in a marked manner by the King. . . . When, on the reception of the deputies, he avoided speaking to me—when, in the receiving line, after speaking to everyone in turn, he broke off immediately he came to me, turned his back, or strolled away across the room—I considered myself justified in supposing that my attitude as a royalist hotspur had exceeded the limits which the King had fixed for himself.

If Frederick William personally avoided too close a contact with Bismarck, there was no such hesitation among his courtiers. He became the close associate of a very influential court clique headed by two brothers, Leopold von Gerlach, a general and an adjutant to the King, and Ludwig von Gerlach, the presiding judge of the highest Prussian tribunal. These men, all of an extreme conservative persuasion, made politics of their own. By secret manipulations they tried to achieve what their ruler had no courage to put into effect by his royal orders. Bismarck became their front man who, in his inflammatory utterances, brought before the public what they had secretly plotted. So the Pomeranian Junker wielded influence and received publicity far beyond what one could usually expect from a newcomer to the political scene.

The Diet adjourned for the summer. Otto sat in front of the Schönhausen manor looking over the rolling fields. In the distance the peasants were moving slowly along the yellow rows, the men swinging their scythes and the women gathering up the sheaves in bundles. It was a pretty sight. Bismarck enjoyed it more now since he had nothing to do with the supervision of the harvest. As a full-time politician he had no desire to play the gentleman farmer any longer. All the farmland had been leased out. Only the garden remained for his pleasure, and his eyes moved approvingly over the neatly cut hedges and the geometrically edged flower beds. Pagan gods of sandstone, shaped by some second-rate sculptor, stood on their pedestals guarding the pathways.

The scene was peaceful. Otto had tasted it with gusto on the first and the second day of his summer vacation. But now it was the end of the first week, and there was no getting around the fact that he was profoundly bored. After the rough-and-tumble of Berlin, the days were long and empty despite the riding and shooting.

Absentmindedly he turned the pages of a book while suppressing a yawn. A messenger brought a stiff card embossed in gold. The Junker glanced at it, then tossed it aside. "Another invitation to a neighbor's dinner party," he moaned. "Those dreadful affairs, those empty-headed country dullards."

But what else was there to do of an evening? He looked at the card again. "Let's see who is the host this time. Herr von Thadden, hmm. Not a bad fellow, but hepped on religion. They will probably pray more than drink. But he has a pretty daughter. Guess I'll look in."

He went, he looked in, and he found himself face to face with a deeply moving drama. Over thirty years old, he was still a bachelor. Just recently he had wooed a young aristocratic lady from an estate not far away only to be rejected by her mother. No man with the reputation of the Mad Junker was acceptable to her as a son-in-law.

Marie von Thadden was not a ravishing beauty. She had the sturdy build of country women. Yet Otto could not turn his eyes from her face, which radiated a profound peace. The gathering had little in common with the usual revelries of the nobility. First Herr von Thadden led the group in a long fervent prayer. Otto observed guests moving their lips in silence, their eyes shining with a great inner involvement. Then came readings from the Bible followed by an earnest discussion of the passages. Obviously every word of the Scriptures was here considered the unalterable truth. Several guests told with much emotion, even with tears, how they once had led sinful lives, but how an overwhelming inner experience had changed them and brought them abiding faith. Now they felt blissfully content and completely assured that they had been saved from eternal damnation.

Among them sat the cynical politician who had not uttered a prayer since early boyhood, whose creed was to fight for what he wanted by fair means or foul. First he felt like laughing, but slowly the atmosphere of the gathering had its effect. A strange mood took hold of him. Was it the girl with her ardent faith or the whole mystic situation into which he had been thrown? Suddenly the big man was crying into his red whiskers.

The Thadden group was part of the pietistic movement which had its beginning in the eighteenth century. These people were all members of the Lutheran religion, Prussia's state church, but they felt the need for a deeper experience than the stiff church services and the cold academic sermons could offer them. They met in private circles where they practiced a deeply personal faith which permeated all their actions and their relations with their fellowmen. In rural Eastern Prussia, this serious religious revival attracted quite a few well-educated idealists.

Bismarck became a regular visitor to the von Thadden house. He felt himself strongly attracted to Marie, and there was no doubt that the young woman was deeply impressed by the tall squire with the ready irreverent wit. For the first time in his life, Otto felt more than a physical desire for a woman. They went on long walks, and the hours were filled with a serious communion of thoughts. Marie made a most sincere vow to "save" the brilliant man with the sinful record, and Otto, for once, kept the dagger of cynicism sheathed. To the girl he revealed a soul tortured by emptiness, a soul hungering for a deeper purpose in life.

This love could not be quenched when he found out that Marie had been, for some time, engaged to Moritz von Blankenburg, an old schoolmate of his. At an earlier time such knowledge might not have deterred him from further advances, but now both he and Marie considered the pledge to Moritz sacred. After she became Frau von Blankenburg, the strange spiritual friendship continued, much to the delight of the Pomeranian Junkers' wives who discovered in it a topic for endless gossip.

Later in the summer Marie arranged an excursion to the famous Harz Mountains. Otto was invited to join the young couple and the bride's parents on this trip, and so was Johanna von Puttkamer, one of Marie's close friends. In two carriages the party traveled through the picturesque valleys which offered glimpses of majestic bald peaks. Legend and literature have celebrated them as the gathering places of witches who come riding on their broomsticks from all corners of the world on the night of the summer solstice.

It was a marvelously refreshing trip. Otto felt at peace as he had never felt before. And it wasn't all prayer and Bible reading either, though there was plenty of both. There were picnics by gushing streams and hikes to the tops of hills which offered splendid views. Poetry was read, and songs rose to the clear summer sky. Marie saw to it that the Junker from Schönhausen spent as much time as possible with Johanna, a petite girl with raven-black hair and gray eyes.

At first Otto felt like scoffing at these obvious attempts at matchmaking. But it was so much like Marie to promote, in this way, the happiness of the man she secretly loved. Since he could never be more than a friend to her, she wanted to lead him to another woman, a substitute for herself, who would help him be strong and abiding in the faith which was so dear to her.

Otto found in Johanna a pleasant and intelligent partner for conversation, no less deeply attached to the pietistic ways than Marie herself, but more sentimental and retiring. He continued to see both of them as often as he could, but his heart belonged to the one who was unattainable.

These new contacts left undeniable impressions on a mind deeply troubled by the lack of spiritual goals. Otto began to read devotional tracts and to carry a Bible on all his travels. In Bismarck's speeches and writings, God was mentioned very frequently, but this newly won interest in religion did not carry over into his methods of dealing with people. There was little of universal love and charity in his personal creed. However, from then on he was convinced that whatever he wanted to do was God's will. Otherwise, why would He have put those desires into his mind? It was comforting to have the Almighty always rooting in one's own corner. "I am God's soldier," he said, "and I must go where He sends me. I believe that He sends me and fashions my life as He needs it." God seemed to send him where Bismarck wanted to go all along.

In the autumn tragedy struck. A vicious epidemic swept the countryside. It began as influenza and swiftly turned into an inflammation of the brain for which medical science knew no cure. Marie was one of its many victims. Bismarck rushed to her bedside. The case was hopeless, yet in the face of death she radiated calmness and profound peace. With her emaciated fingers she clasped his huge hand. "I have prayed so ardently that God may bring you and Johanna together, that together you may seek Him out through the long years of your lives."

Her death shook him to the foundations of his being. In a letter to Johanna's father he confessed that he had cried long and hard and that, for the first time, he had turned to God in prayer:

> When Marie lay dying the first fervent prayer had burst forth from my heart without any brooding on my part on whether or no it was contrary to reason. My prayer remained unheard, yet it had not been rejected, for I have never again lost the ability to petition Him, and though I have no sense of peace, yet I feel within me confidence and a zest of life to a degree which I have never previously experienced.

This letter, one of the finest products of his considerable literary talent, was the missive in which Bismarck asked for the hand of

Johanna von Puttkamer. Though it has the ring of sincerity, historians have argued ever since how much of its contents reflects real feeling and how much was the product of clever diplomacy designed to overcome the notoriety of the Mad Junker and to make his proposal acceptable.

Whatever the intent, it worked. Otto and Johanna were married in July 1847. He had developed genuine affection for his delicate bride, but the picture of Marie remained enshrined in his memory with an intensity that knew no rival.

Never given to personal economizing, he took his young wife on a long and costly honeymoon. Only first-rate hotels and the posh meeting places of high society would do. It was a splendid tour with many fascinating stops, but the high point came when they reached Venice, the Mecca of European newlyweds of means.

One evening at the theater he discovered that the center box was occupied by none other than his own sovereign, who was enjoying a little vacation from his monarchical duties. He bowed deeply toward the box, and Frederick William, recognizing him, answered with a gracious wave of the royal hand. Next morning the Junker received at his hotel an invitation to dine with the King. This was a pleasant surprise considering the snubs he had endured back in Berlin. His pleasure was only temporarily dimmed by the discovery that he had not taken along the formal clothing appropriate for such an occasion, and there was no time to engage the services of a local tailor. But the King seemed oblivious to this breach of court etiquette. Almost gloatingly Bismarck wrote of the event:

> My reception was so kindly, and the conversation, even on political subjects, of such a nature as to enable me to infer that my attitude in the Diet met with his encouraging approval. The King commanded me to call on him in the course of the winter. . . . I became persuaded that I stood high in the favor of the King. . . .

At the end of the memorable evening, as he bowed himself respectfully out of the royal presence, he felt that he had just received the most precious wedding gift of all. The future looked bright.

✠ 4 ✠

BLOOD MUST FLOW

THE MARCH WINDS IN 1848 WERE RAW AND BITING. ON THE Pomeranian plains spring was still only a gentle hope. A group of Junkers and their ladies were passing the time in the parlor of an East Elbian estate. Reclining on the fading silk of rococo couches, they exchanged small talk between sips of champagne from cut crystal glasses. Looking ahead to the summer, they talked of the resorts and casinos they were going to visit. Bismarck was among the guests.

Curious noises made them turn toward the window. A carriage, pitifully spattered with mud, had halted in the oval driveway. Several fashionably dressed women alighted. They supported each other as if about to faint from exhaustion. Driven by curiosity Bismarck stormed out into the front court. He recognized the women as members of the nobility.

Obviously they were completely upset. They babbled all at the same time so that it was hard to understand them. "Revolution in Berlin . . ." that much he could make out.

Finally they quieted down enough to speak a little more coherently:

"There were giant demonstrations. We heard shooting in the streets. They are building barricades."

"The King is in the hands of the rebels."

"The soldiers have withdrawn to Potsdam."

Vainly Bismarck tried to extract from the distraught women more precise information. They could not tell anything further, except that some nobles had been badly beaten and they were afraid for their lives.

As the refugees were led away to receive the hospitality of the house, he was already astride his horse. The fighting cock was smelling the scent of blood.

Within a few short hours he sat on a train bound for Berlin. Impatiently he squirmed on the hard wooden bench of the rickety contraption which puffed with painfully slow pace through the dreary countryside. Only a short time earlier, the railroad had made its appearance in Prussia. Even had the passenger felt less pressed for time, the ride in the soot-coated compartment would have been far from pleasurable. The rattling was infernal, and the air was stale.

As there was no way to speed up the journey, he settled back and made himself as comfortable as possible. Closing his red-rimmed eyes, he reviewed the situation. The outbreak of violence had not come as a complete surprise.

The smell of rebellion was in the air, not only in Prussia but over much of the continent. Half a century ago, the French Revolution, with its battle cry, "Liberty, Fraternity, Equality," had roused hopes for a better life everywhere. It had promised freedom from the arbitrary rule of absolute monarchs. Napoleon's soldiers had carried the message from land to land. Frightened princes hastily promised all sorts of democratic innovations. But after their loyal armies had driven out Napoleon's forces, no more was heard of those promises.

Members of the middle class, especially the students and their professors, were smarting under narrow governmental suppression, under restrictions of speech and learning. Since open protests were impossible, smoldering sentiments were kindled by secret literature smuggled across frontiers. In clandestine meetings revolutionary spokesmen preached the twin gospels of liberalism and nationalism. Both these movements were directed against a common enemy: autocratic rulers who denied their subjects all rights, including the right to unite with others who spoke the same language or the right to be independent from enslavement by a foreign nationality.

Early in the year 1848, thousands took to the streets in Paris,

Vienna and Prague, in the cities of Hungary and Italy. There were uprisings in many German states. Merchants, artisans, students marched on the seats of government, accompanied by a sprinkling of factory workers. With a demand for personal liberty and constitutional rights they coupled the wish for a united Germany. There was a general desire to be rid of the many princes, most of whom were petty, indolent tyrants. To the inhabitants of Hesse, Baden, Saxony and all the other German states, including Prussia, the words "Germany" and "freedom" had become synonymous.

On paper there existed already something which could be taken for an all-German national organization. The Congress of Vienna had established a German Federation with a permanent Federal Diet meeting in the city of Frankfort-on-the-Main. Both Austria and Prussia were members of the federation. But the German people had nothing to do with all this. The Federal Diet was merely a representation of the thirty-nine German princes. Their personal ambassadors were the ones who made up the Diet, acting only upon instructions from their own sovereigns. Moreover, the Austrian envoy was the permanent president of their sessions; he completely dominated the proceedings.

National feeling among Germans in all walks of life had reached a peak. They demanded unity without waiting for their reluctant rulers, who feared to lose their little thrones. United action had also emerged on the economic front, as a matter of prudence and of sheer necessity. The *Zollverein* (customs union), founded in 1819, eliminated tariffs between individual states. Goods could now move freely to markets from one end of Germany to the other. This helped stimulate unprecedented economic growth in an area which had long lagged behind western Europe. While Austria was firmly in control of the Federal Diet, Prussia was the leading member of the *Zollverein*. In fact, she consistently refused to grant her chief rival admission in the customs union. The showdown between the two powerful contenders for German leadership was shaping up.

Practically everybody was for unification, but on the "how" of bringing the states together opinions were deeply divided. Conserva-

3

tives on the whole favored the *grossdeutsche* (large German) solution, which would make Austria part of the new German nation. This would give the Habsburgs a leading position despite the fact that their domain contained millions of non-German people.

Liberals were more inclined toward a *kleindeutsche* (small German) entity with the exclusion of Austria. Freedom-loving Germans held a passionate hatred for the Habsburg regime, which they denounced as the most brutal police state in Europe, surpassed only by Russia. The very name of Prince Klemens von Metternich, the Austrian chancellor, had become a symbol of choking reactionary oppression.

Then there was Otto von Bismarck, in a class all by himself. He wanted nothing to do with "the German swindle," as he called it. For the moment he refused to see farther than to the borders of his own Prussia.

At the depot of a little provincial town the train ground to a painful halt, sputtering and groaning as if about to fall apart. On the platform newsboys were yelling, "Extra, extra. King gives in to rebels. Extra, extra."

In an involuntary gesture Bismarck clenched his fists. So those hysterical women were right after all. He called one of the boys. According to the papers, the revolution was victorious. There had been giant street demonstrations in Berlin. Before the royal palace, soldiers had fired into the crowd, whereupon barricades went up all over the city. As the disciplined troops and the furious Berliners faced each other, the King decided to humor the rebels. He did not want to go down in history as a bloody butcher of his own people. With a black-red-gold cockade, the emblem of a united Germany, on his hat, he marched in the funeral procession which carried the victims of his soldiers' bullets. Then he ordered the regiments out of the city. "I have never been safer," he solemnly declared, "than under the protection of my good citizens."

The Junker bit his lips in rage. "So the King is a prisoner in his own palace," he muttered. "The fool. A few more salvos into the rabble, and the whole revolution would have been over."

At the Berlin railroad station he looked anxiously around. Almost everybody wore the black-red-gold emblem. Nobody paid him any attention. An aristocratic friend with whom he had emptied many a goblet walked right past him without giving any sign of recognition.

"So that is the way it goes," Bismarck thought grimly. It was a dangerous place for one with the reputation of being the most implacable foe of popular reform. No wonder the nobleman did not want to be seen with him.

Nervously he ducked into the barbershop across from the station. The red whiskers fell under the shears. At a street corner he bought an all-German cockade, and with a grimace of disgust he pinned it to his broad-brimmed hat. Then he was off to the palace.

"Nobody can see the King," said the guard at the gate. "Please move on, sir."

"But I have to. It is of the utmost importance."

"Sorry. I have my orders." That was the end of the discussion. Bismarck repeated his plea to the lieutenant of the guard, with the same result. The officer finally permitted him to write a note on a scrap of paper in the guardroom. An orderly disappeared with it into the interior of the cavernous building. Gnawing his mustache which the barber had saved, Otto waited for hours. There was no response.

"It is as I feared. He is a prisoner. He must be liberated from the outside."

The man whom so many hated for his cold, cynical manners turned into a quixotic figure, trembling, crying, raging in convulsive fits. Reason seemed to have left him.

He returned to Schönhausen and called upon his peasants to arm themselves. In his imagination he pictured a huge host of loyal country people marching against the debased city mob. From all corners of the manor he collected shotguns and ancient pistols. Servants were dispatched to fetch gunpowder from the nearest town. Not understanding what it was all about, the plowmen and sheepherders enjoyed the break in their monotonous routine.

From the town came emissaries to hoist the black-red-gold colors over the village. Brandishing their weapons the peasants drove them off. Then their squire personally raised the black Prussian flag with the white cross in the center.

With his wife beside him, he rode all over the neighborhood making patriotic appeals. This was parochial Prussian, not German patriotism, of course. With endless references to honor and duty he called for enlistment in his counterrevolutionary army.

At one estate he ran into a landlord with more liberal notions who declared, "I will speak after you and argue against you."

"Then I will shoot you down, sir," was the quick reply.

"No, you won't do that."

"I give you my word of honor. You know that I always keep my word. So leave this nonsense."

The neighbor obeyed, at least till the irate Junker was out of sight.

Again Bismarck took the train. He alighted at Potsdam where the Berlin garrison was encamped. The generals whom he knew personally were more accessible than the King. Patiently they listened to his plan for liberating the monarch with the help of his tenant army. A high staff officer spoke to him as one reasons with a wild-eyed child, "What we need is grain and potatoes for the troops not peasants."

The whole idea was ridiculous. Besides, a Prussian officer never acted without orders from his superiors.

Failing to rouse the military into action, Bismarck turned to other schemes as if it were up to him to save the Prussian monarchy single-handedly. Since the King was deprived of his liberty, he reasoned, the Prussian throne was actually vacant. Somebody else had to take over the royal powers. He wanted to approach Prince William, the King's brother, who would be the logical substitute. But the Prince was nowhere to be found. At the first news of unrest he had gone into hiding on an island off the coast. From there he sailed to England to wait out the storm.

Undismayed, Bismarck promoted the abdication of the King in favor of Prince William's young son, Frederick. The only effect of all this feverish activity was that he made a lifelong enemy of William's wife, the Princess Augusta. Nor was the King himself too pleased when he heard of those underhanded machinations.

In 1848 Bismarck displayed a degree of immaturity in judgment which is astounding in the light of his later accomplishments. In his defense it can be said that he was then an outsider without any responsibilities. One could not expect from him the restraint that comes with the assumption of important obligations.

Cooler heads prevailed in the end. Violent action which would have been disastrous for everybody was avoided. No peasants with shotguns, no volleys fired by regulars were needed to put down the revolution. It died of its own inertia, not only in Berlin but all over Europe. With army and bureaucracy as its reliable props, the centralized state triumphed everywhere. The commercial class was anxious to get back to the business of making money, intellectuals were split into many factions, while the laboring man and the peasant had more pressing needs than a constitution.

Bismarck was disappointed that not more rebel blood had been spilled in the streets. To provoke the masses into a frenzy of violence and then teach them a lesson with guns and bayonets was the strategy he would have favored.

Again the monarchs asserted themselves with the help of police and censors. Reaction was once more in the saddle. However, the wheels of history never turn backward for long. During the following decades, the autocratic fetters were gradually loosened, and a modest measure of democratic procedure was introduced everywhere, even in Prussia.

The King finally granted a constitution. It was not what the liberals had demanded, and it bore little resemblance to the great document under which the United States is governed. Still it was a concession to the will of the people. The constitution provided for general elections to a Parliament, but the hereditary monarch retained the power to make all important decisions. The cabinet ministers were responsible only to him and served at his pleasure. This type of government, parliamentary in form but autocratic in substance, remained typical for Germany as long as the monarchy existed there.

The army remained the stoutest pillar of state authority. On several occasions, Prussian troops were even dispatched outside their own territory to suppress democratic insurgents in other states, particularly in Saxony and Baden. No wonder the Prussian uniform was hated far and wide as the cloth of diehard despotism.

Even the mild concessions to popular will were too much for Bismarck's taste, and he felt no reluctance saying so publicly. Nor did he hesitate telling the monarch himself to his face that he considered him a spineless weakling.

After all the revolutionary excitement was over, he was finally granted a royal audience. He found the King and the Queen on the terrace which overlooked an enormous artificial pool. Barely observing the niceties required by court etiquette, he reproached the sovereign for his softness during the stormy March days.

"How can you talk like this to your king?" interrupted the outraged Queen.

"Let him talk, Elizabeth. Exactly on what account are you reproaching me, Herr von Bismarck?"

"That you gave up Berlin rather than fight for it."

Again the Queen intervened. "You cannot blame the King for that. He had not slept for three days."

"A king *must* be able to sleep," was the insolent answer.

Elections for the new Parliament were scheduled. Bismarck coveted a seat badly, not because he liked Parliament, but because he needed a base of operation for his enormous political ambitions. But no district wanted him for a candidate, not even his own home territory. Finally he managed to run for office in a distant part of Brandenburg province where he owed the nomination to the local prison warden, whose wife was related to Johanna.

Swallowing his contempt for the common man, he went on the campaign trail. His election was secured by a hair-thin majority. The townspeople had solidly rejected him. Only with the help of the landed gentry and of a lopsided electoral system did he squeeze by. Again the whirlpool of parliamentary debate and backstage intrigue swallowed him completely. Though his time was taken up with speeches, conferences and article writing, he thrived in this bracing atmosphere. Before coming to Berlin, he had been plagued by frequent stomach upsets and fits of melancholy. Now his health seemed perfect though he continued to eat and drink enormous quantities. His midriff began to show the effects of such feasting, and under the newly grown side-whiskers his cheeks were round and rosy.

Of all the political issues, those which excited him the most dealt with foreign relations. This interest grew over the years to an all-consuming passion.

Prussia's foreign policy began with her relations to the other German states. The problem of unification continued to be on everybody's mind. Under the impact of the 1848 Revolution, a number of distinguished men from all corners of Germany had gathered in Frankfort, the seat of the Federal Diet, and declared themselves to be the first all-German parliament. Many inspiring speeches were heard in St. Paul's Church where they met. An air of high idealism and romantic fervor prevailed. But when it came to the details of the future national governmental machinery, the planning bogged down in endless debate.

Not until the following year, after the general revolutionary ardor had cooled, was it decided in Frankfort that the new Germany should have a liberal constitution, yet should be headed by an emperor, a *Kaiser*. The Frankfort Assembly also declared itself for the *kleindeutsche* solution. Accordingly, a delegation of lawyers and academicians appeared at the royal palace in Berlin and solemnly offered Frederick William IV the crown of a German Empire which was still an idea, not a reality.

The Hohenzollern King was flattered, asked for time to think it over, then refused. At the height of the Berlin rebellion he had echoed the demands of his people by declaring, "Prussia will merge into Germany." Now he answered the delegation from Frankfort, "I will not take the imperial crown from the gutter. Only the princes of Germany can rightfully offer it to me." He preferred no Germany to one tainted with democracy.

After this rejection, the Frankfort Assembly soon withered away and finally died an inglorious death. The Federal Diet, which had been temporarily eclipsed by it, made a comeback. It still was no more than a council of princely envoys.

One man who heartily approved his sovereign's brusque rejection of the German crown was Otto von Bismarck. In speech after speech he asserted that his only political aim was a more powerful Prussia and his only loyalty to the Hohenzollern dynasty. "We are Prussians," he screamed in his shrill voice, "and I hope to God that Prussians will remain Prussians long after the Frankfort constitution has mouldered away like a withered autumn leaf." He knew that a greater Germany would, of necessity, have to be a more liberal Germany. For this reason alone he wanted none of it.

In 1850 his government got into an argument with Austria over their respective roles in other parts of Germany. Threats were issued and sabers rattled. In the officers' messes there was talk of impending action. But far from showing the warlike spirit he had exhibited two years earlier, Bismarck came out strongly for avoiding armed conflict with Austria. This bulwark of reaction should be imitated, not attacked. He warmly applauded his government when, in the humiliating Treaty of Olmütz, it gave in to all Austrian demands. The Prussians promised to be docile and to refrain from displeasing the house of Habsburg from now on.

Berlin had become Bismarck's real home. Its high-tension atmosphere, the rumors, the military displays and royal functions made it a place full of fascination. Otto and Johanna took a modest ground-floor apartment on Behrenstrasse and furnished it with minute care. His tastes continued to be expensive, and cash was still in short supply.

Johanna was much less impressed with life in the capital city. She did not understand the intricacies of high politics, nor did she make any effort to learn. Her husband insisted that she take up horseback riding and the study of foreign languages so that she would acquire the polish expected from a society lady. But though she loved Otto deeply and was completely awed by his brilliance, she refused to play the part in which he wanted to cast her. For long spells she absented herself from their apartment and stayed with her parents in the country. The reason given was poor health, from which she suffered all her life. One extended absence was prompted by her first confinement. In 1848 their daughter was born and named Marie, in memory of the woman who had brought them together. In the following year she gave birth to their oldest son, Herbert.

The letters Johanna received from her husband were treasures of style and poetic feeling. In simple but moving word pictures he expressed his loneliness. Inadvertently he slipped into politics, the subject which consumed all his waking hours, only to apologize after a few paragraphs for boring her with matters which held no attraction for her.

From the most sarcastic jabs at public figures the letters slid into exquisite miniatures full of charm:

> Yesterday we had soft, warm autumn weather, and I took a long walk in the *Tiergarten* [a park in Berlin], by the same solitary paths which we used to traverse together. I sat, too, on our bench near the swan pond. The young swans which were then still in their eggs on the little island were now swimming vivaciously about, fat, gray and blasé, among the dirty ducks, and the old ones sleepily laid their heads on their backs. The handsome large maple standing near the bridge already has leaves of a dark-red color. I wished to send you one, but in my pocket it has become so hard that it crumbles away. The pond is almost dried up. The lindens, the black alders and other delicate things bestrew the path with their yellow rustling foliage, and the round chestnut burrs exhibit a medley of all shades of sombre and attractive fall coloring. . . .

This from the man who was held to be without pity and without tact, whose very name caused people to shudder with revulsion.

His mind was a web of complicated and contradictory strains, but overriding all was the yearning for power. The speeches in the legislative halls and the activities in the cloakrooms were still only preliminaries. Bismarck was impatiently awaiting bigger opportunities. Quite unashamedly he badgered his friends in high places to help him obtain a cabinet post. More than once, when a ministerial shake-up was ordered, his influential mentor, Leopold von Gerlach, proposed his name to the King. But every time the royal pen scratched it from the list. "A red reactionary thirsting for blood. Only to be used when the bayonet reigns supremely": thus read Frederick William's marginal note of refusal. Was it Bismarck's political notoriety or the King's personal dislike which prompted such notes? Probably it was both.

The Junker continued to wait and to pull strings. At long last the break came in 1851. His Majesty finally conceded that this zealous super-royalist had to be given some token of appreciation, preferably one which would take him away from the capital. At the age of thirty-six, Otto von Bismarck found himself posted to Frankfort. He had been made Prussian envoy to the Federal Diet.

Court protocol required that he come to the royal palace to express his personal thanks for this, his first diplomatic appointment. He was told by the King, "You are a bold man to take a foreign post like this without previous experience."

"I have courage enough to obey, if Your Majesty has courage enough to command."

This was true Bismarckian style.

✠ 5 ✠

JUNKER DIPLOMAT

COUNT THUN, THE AUSTRIAN ENVOY TO THE GERMAN FEDERAL Diet, relaxed in his overstuffed armchair smoking a long, thin Havana cigar. The delegates from the other German states stood around conversing in low voices. It was Bismarck's first session since his appointment as the Prussian representative to Frankfort.

The Prussian cut a good figure in this exclusive gathering. His diplomatic uniform still had the sheen of newness. The golden stripes running down each trouser leg shone brightly. The gold-embroidered black jacket fitted snugly over the white waistcoat and the silken shirt. A black tie was wound several times around the murderously high collar. Taller than anybody else in the white-and-gold hall, he stroked his well-trimmed whiskers.

"Why aren't we sitting down?" he asked one of his colleagues from a smaller state. "What are these for?" He pointed to the chairs neatly arranged around a huge polished oak table.

"Only the Austrian sits. We others wait till he gives the sign which opens the meeting. And nobody else smokes when he is around. It is quite a custom."

"Then a change of custom is in order," grumbled the Prussian. He planted himself in a chair right next to the Austrian count. Then he pulled a golden case from his pocket and carefully selected one of his imported cigars. "May I trouble you for a light, Herr Count?" he asked innocently. "I seem to have forgotten my matches at home."

Startled, but without losing his composure, Count Thun complied. The session began with the reading of the minutes. Bismarck interrupted, "From all I have heard about the last meeting, the minutes are not correct. The presiding envoy from Austria must have altered the record."

The Count's face flushed, and the monocle dropped from his right eye. "If that record is not correct, I am a liar."

"Exactly so, Your Excellency." The answer was cold and clipped.

A deadly silence settled over the chamber. Nobody had ever spoken to the president like this. According to the aristocratic code, only a challenge to armed combat could be the proper response. But Thun decided to treat the matter in the manner of an adult. He pretended not to have heard the insult. The meeting went on. To everyone present it was obvious that a new era had begun for the Federal Diet.

Bismarck had arrived at his post as a friend of reactionary Austria. In fact, this was why his arch-conservative patrons at court had recommended him. But almost immediately his outlook changed drastically. As an ambassador he was supposed to be only the mouthpiece of his government, but soon Bismarck began to make policies of his own. Never mind the dispatches from Berlin.

Here, amidst the wire pulling, the leaked secrets and the skilled spying, he had found a field of activity worthy of his talents and of his inclinations. The small-time hometown politician was dead. The master diplomat was coming to life.

He was still the same tradition-minded Junker he had always been, hostile to any popular expression, but his mind was now occupied by loftier designs. Disdainfully he snorted at party programs and political philosophies. Labels meant nothing to him anymore. In his own words, "in politics no one does anything for another, unless he finds it also in his own interest to do so."

Not by accident did he often compare diplomacy with a game of chess. He himself became the champion chess player, adept at clever planning, at outmaneuvering and outguessing his opponents. Unscrupulously he employed any trick that would lead to the desired checkmate. But while the professional chess player remains cool and detached during the game, Bismarck never forgave any personal slight.

The Federal Diet was an outdated piece of machinery. The envoys pretended to act as representatives of independent rulers while, in reality, their princes were the puppets of the only sizable powers: Austria and Prussia.

Austria's ill-disguised intention was to use the Diet as an instrument for the domination of all German lands. Bismarck was determined to prevent this. If Prussia was to acquire strength and command the respect of other strong powers, Austria had to be humbled. It was a case of irrefutable logic. "Germany," he wrote in a famous state paper, "is too small for both of us. Both plow the same contested field. . . . Only a war will put right the clock of Germany's development."

Soon he had occasion to begin his relentless drive of putting Austria in her place. He successfully torpedoed her admission to the *Zollverein* when the time came to extend the life of the German customs union. The Viennese government had dearly wanted to become a member, but had to look on helplessly as Bismarck's clever machinations closed the door.

Without hesitation he set to work to destroy the whole institution of the Federal Diet because Austria controlled it. That Prussia was one of its members did not deter him. Soon he was dreaded and hated not only by the Austrians but also by all their smaller satellites. They were no match for his biting insolence.

As earlier in Berlin, he coldly ignored the hatred around him. Stones were thrown at him in the streets of Frankfort. The press condemned him almost solidly. He countered with icy contempt that all journalists could be bought if the price was right.

But his days in Frankfort were not all grim and filled with verbal combat. The city on the Main River, not far from its confluence with the Rhine, was peculiarly fitted for an all-German gathering. Here north met south, and the various dialects blended into a mellow idiom. In its city hall the medieval German emperors had been elected, and in the majestic cathedral nearby they had been crowned. This municipality came as close as it was possible to being the German capital.

Now the diplomats and their entourages occupied many stately townhouses and the more pretentious villas in the outskirts. The Bismarcks had rented a spacious home with lots of rooms for the cooks and footmen. On his king's birthday Otto gave a sumptuous dinner dance for three hundred guests. He still spent more than he could afford, but now he felt that the stinginess of the envoy would reflect unfavorably on his government.

Receptions and balls in unending succession were part of the diplomatic life. Bismarck participated not only out of a sense of duty, but also because he enjoyed it tremendously. The gentlemen were impressed by his expert knowledge of French and Rhenish wines, and the ladies in their gorgeous diamond-studded gowns admired his clever repartee. Again he had his whiskers shaved off, leaving only the famous bushy mustache. This time the intention was not disguise, but to impress the ladies of Frankfort.

The gruff violator of all polite conventions could be a charming conversationalist. Widely read and widely traveled, a keen observer and clear thinker, he towered high above his colleagues who had little to recommend them except their titles.

He displayed no genuine affection for anybody. Even the love he gave his own family was based on his role as the undisputed patriarch. Johanna kept house, but stayed away from the balls and soirées. Whatever her Otto did was right, as far as she was concerned. Whatever unkind things were said about him, came from evil mouths.

A second son was born in 1852. Prince William consented to be his godfather. The boy was named after him, but his father always called him Bill, perhaps out of his lifelong fondness of British ways.

The meetings of the Diet droned on. Most of the time no definite action resulted, thanks to Bismarck's tactics of obstruction. He amused himself by making hair-splitting objections to everything the Austrians proposed, but when the arguments became heated, he always managed to pose as the injured party.

Frequently he boarded the train for Berlin, where he closeted himself with General von Gerlach and other advisers to the King or even with the royal master himself. Though he was only one of many Prussian ambassadors, he was sent for much more frequently than others. Such was the value placed on his judgment.

Often he did not even wait for a summons, but came on his own initiative when he felt the government was headed in the wrong direction and needed to be set straight. In between trips he bombarded the capital with memoranda. They were not the usual reports required of ambassadors, but unsolicited dissertations of his views on foreign policy. The Minister of Foreign Affairs, Baron von Manteuffel, who was his superior, did not take kindly to such independent moves by one of his ambassadors. But Bismarck, otherwise such a stern advocate of authority and discipline, continued cheerfully to go over his head.

He had long realized that Prussia's fate was inseparably linked, not only with developments inside the German pale, but also with events which happened far beyond it. He became a keen observer of the worldwide political scene, and what he saw caused him grave concern. The storm clouds were dark and menacing.

The year 1854 marked the beginning of the Crimean War, a conflict between Russia, on the one hand, and Turkey, France and England, on the other. Russia was pursuing her old dream of an outlet to the Mediterranean Sea, and her enemies were determined to prevent this. Over two years of murderous fighting ended with Russia's humiliation and with the emergence of the two Western powers as the leading imperialistic countries.

Prussia had the wisdom to stay out of this conflict. Much of the credit goes to Bismarck, who had assessed the situation correctly. The incessant stream of his dispatches to the capital did much to overcome the strong desire of many influential Prussians to participate in the armed clash. It would have rent the state asunder, for the liberals were all for attacking Russia, the epitome of cruel despotism, whereas the conservatives favored her for the same reasons. Besides, the Czar was a close relative of the Prussian King.

Only three years after the end of this war, European armies were again locked in combat. This time France combined with tiny Sardinia to challenge Austria. Again Prussian sentiments were divided, and tempers rose high. Despite the many differences, it was felt that Germans should stand together in times of danger and, therefore, that Austria should be supported. But there were those who admired Cavour, the ingenious prime minister of Sardinia, who, with this war, spearheaded the unification of Italy. Like Germany, Italy was still broken into many parts, several of them dominated by the Habsburgs.

Once more Bismarck counseled neutrality, and his counsel prevailed. Since members of the German Federation were supposed to come to each other's aid, negotiations were begun with Austria about the dispatching of Prussian troops. Bismarck managed to drag out the proceedings, and the war ended before any agreement was reached. Probably Vienna feared the friendly Prussian regiments more than it did the enemy.

The man from Schönhausen had demonstrated that he was not a single-minded militarist like so many of his fellow Junkers, who could see the solution of a controversy only through the barrel of a rifle. He felt that war was necessary only as an extended instrument of diplomacy. The right course to follow was always the one which would most enhance the power of the state. No wars should be fought because of likes or dislikes or out of gratitude, honor or revenge.

I draw my attitude toward foreign powers not from stagnant antipathies, but only from usefulness or hurtfulness for Prussia. . . . Beware of sentimental alliances where the consciousness of good deeds is the only compensation for noble sacrifices.

This is the essence of Bismarck's famous *realpolitik* (politics of realism), which strongly calls to mind the ideas proffered, about three hundred years earlier, by Niccolo Machiavelli in *The Prince*. But whereas the Italian author had to confine his thoughts to the written page, Bismarck's opportunity eventually came to act his out.

While the Prussian ambassador was aggravating his colleagues in Frankfort, critical days followed one another in Berlin. King Frederick William IV had lapsed into the darkness of complete insanity. Even the most stubborn royalists had to concede that he was now unable to perform his functions. He abdicated, and his brother became regent. In 1861 a stroke ended Frederick's life, which had stood so long under the growing shadow of mental derangement.

Bismarck rushed home for the coronation of William I. In his blue reserve officer's uniform he stood amidst the splendid gathering of notables and burghers, all costumed in the luster of past centuries. The sounds of blaring trumpets mingled with the gentle tolling of church bells. Freshly polished medieval weaponry, flags and streamers, coats of arms, the kerchiefs of peasant girls—all combined into a riotous symphony of color.

The new King was sixty-three years old. He carried himself stiffly erect like the soldier he had been all his life. Neatly rounded white whiskers covered his cheeks leaving the chin bare, the fashion among distinguished elderly gentlemen.

Robed in purple and gold, William strode slowly into the semidarkness of the cathedral followed by representatives of the highest nobility carrying the Hohenzollern sword and shield. A hymn sung by an invisible choir sounded more like a battle song than a chanted praise of the Creator. The procession halted before the high altar on which rested the golden crown of Prussia. Unaided, William I reached for it and put it on his head. Nobody else was to touch it. He had insisted that this part of the ceremony be carried out in no other way to symbolize that his royal power derived directly from God and not from any human decision. More than any previous Hohenzollern ruler he considered himself appointed by heaven, selected solely through "the grace of God."

Bismarck, now forty-four, had met the new King many times

before. No great love was lost between the two, but in a reserved, formal way, they had been on friendly terms. Both shared an extremely conservative outlook. Being the younger brother of a royal heir-apparent, William had considered it very unlikely that he would ever occupy a throne, and little had been done to prepare him for such a task. He had devoted himself wholeheartedly to the military life, and he represented all the good and bad qualities of Prussian militarism. His honesty and sense of duty were beyond reproach, but of the world beyond the confines of the parade ground he was profoundly ignorant. His great pride was that he knew all Prussian officers by name. They were his children, and he was their patriarchal master.

With the change of the top command, a deep restlessness had overcome the envoy in Frankfort. His spasms of melancholy and his physical ailments recurred at shorter intervals. He was not about to resign himself to an ambassadorial career. Never was he in any doubt that fate had designated him for a star role on the world stage. Already he was playing a part far weightier than that of the usual diplomatic representative. Most people who knew him expected that, sooner or later, he would be chosen for bigger tasks.

Bismarck made no secret of his desire to get into the cabinet. In fact, in response to his hints and to the suggestions of his influential friends, ministerial posts had been offered him several times under the old King. But each time he had declined. Once he could have become Minister of Finance, but economic matters were not for him. Only one pursuit interested him: to conduct Prussia's foreign affairs.

The time was critical. He was approaching middle age while his new King was an old man who had probably just a few years left to wield the scepter. Perhaps this was the last chance to secure the deeply desired advancement. He redoubled his efforts, openly and behind the scenes, making sure that William I was often reminded of the Junker's unswerving loyalty to the throne.

Yet the King hesitated. Bismarck's notoriety as a troublemaker bothered him. Why start his reign with such an unpopular appointment? Then there were the ambassador's ideas of boosting Prussia's standing in the world. They sounded very attractive, but also very dangerous.

One thing was certain: Bismarck had to be moved from Frankfort to avoid difficulties with the other German states, especially with Austria. With his brusque and often insulting behavior, the Junker had burned his bridges behind him.

A summons came from Berlin. After eight years as ambassador to the German Federal Diet, Bismarck found himself in the royal palace facing his King in private audience. Surely this was the great moment.

William I was unusually friendly. For a while they made small talk about Frankfort society and about the health of both their families. Then came the bombshell.

"Now to your future, my dear Bismarck. Of course, I want you to keep on serving Prussia as vigorously as you have done in the past. I have a most desirable post for you. I am sending you as my ambassador to St. Petersburg."

It was a terrible shock. Bismarck almost forgot that he was in the presence of royalty. "I understand, Your Majesty. I am to be put in cold storage on the Neva River."

"How can you say such a thing? The Russian capital has always been regarded as the top diplomatic post. You should consider this appointment a token of my highest confidence."

By now Bismarck had regained control of himself. "Since Your Majesty makes me this kind of compliment, I must, of course, remain silent."

He had made himself the foremost champion of royal absolutism. Now he was tasting its bitter fruit. The King had spoken. His will must prevail.

✠ 6 ✠

IN COLD STORAGE

WITH MIXED FEELINGS THE NEW AMBASSADOR UNDERTOOK THE five-day journey to the Russian capital. The farther he penetrated the endless cold flatlands of eastern Europe, the more he felt like going into a joyless exile. But once in St. Petersburg, he soon warmed up to the ways of his hosts. The Czar and the high Russian aristocracy lived in a grand style unknown to the more frugal Prussians. Again his tight financial circumstances posed a problem. It was hard to keep up with all the grand dukes and duchesses and with the dashing officers of the guard regiments.

But he did his best, with the usual disregard of the cash balance. The men were impressed by his ability to drink even the most hardened consumers of strong spirits under the table, and in St. Petersburg they knew how to drink. He also held his own at the bear hunts in the endless frozen forests. On wintry sleigh rides he was a gay and gallant companion of the ladies, and at night in the casinos he displayed calm and confidence.

What was much more important, he hit it off with Czar Alexander II, who was a nephew of his own King, and with other members of the Romanov family. The Czar's mother was an invalid who tremendously enjoyed Bismarck's visits. For hours he would sit at her bedside, entertaining her with amusing stories and incidentally receiving all sorts of valuable inside information whch was not available through official channels. He was also on good terms with

Prince Gortschakoff, the Prime Minister, with whom he was to deal frequently in later phases of his life. His anti-Austrian record was a great asset in St. Petersburg; the Russians were quite angry at the Danube monarchy for failing to help them in the Crimean War as it had been expected to do.

It did not take Bismarck long to master the Russian language, thought to move in the leading social circles of the capital his fluent French would have been sufficient. By traveling extensively across the immense empire he made himself thoroughly familiar with its geographical and historical features. Russian officials and fellow envoys considered him by far the best informed member of the diplomatic corps.

His special mission was to maintain friendly relations between his own and the Czarist government, and he applied himself to this task with full inner conviction. Prussia and Russia, he felt, should never be on opposite sides in any conflict. Both were ruled according to authoritarian principles, and neither possessed anything the other wanted. Each intended to grow in size, but not at the expense of the other. He was convinced that an extending Prussia would, sooner or later, have to clash with Austria and France. Therefore it was imperative to keep on good terms with the eastern giant. He wrote: "With France we shall never have peace, with Russia never the necessity of war, unless liberal stupidity or dynastic blunders spoil the situation."

In Berlin the aging King read the dispatches from St. Petersburg with obvious pleasure. This was the kind of adviser he needed, a man whose gift of sharp, penetrating analysis, whose ability to draw up minute but far-reaching plans rose sky-high above anything he could find among his present ministers. He wanted this man closer to home where he could put his phenomenal brainpower to immediate use when he needed it. In March of 1862 the order of recall arrived in the Russian capital.

Bismarck obeyed in haste, leaving behind a household full of books and furniture. He took no time to dismiss the squad of domestics who had served him nor to dispose of the horses and carriages he had acquired. Perhaps this was the great moment. On the other hand, he had been disappointed before and he tried not to raise his hopes too high.

His doubts were justified. Frustration awaited him in Berlin. Days of idleness followed each other without any summons from the King. As always when his mind was condemned to unwanted leisure, he became irritable. Headaches and nervous pains tormented him.

General Albrecht von Roon, the Minister of War and an uncompromising militarist, urged an appointment to a top post for Bismarck. Others close to the throne supported him. Still William I could not make up his mind.

Just then he desperately needed a strong personality in a position of leadership, for he was in deep trouble. The King was an upright man whose given word was as good as gold, but his outlook and his abilities were extremely limited. He was deeply convinced that what Prussia needed before anything else was a powerful army. All other goals paled into insignificance before this aspiration which was so close to his heart.

Urged on by Roon and other generals, he had endorsed a plan to give the military strength of Prussia an extraordinary boost. Draftees had been serving two years. Now the time was to be lengthened to three years, which would increase the number of soldiers under arms by one third. At the same time, the role of the citizen's militia, the *Landwehr,* was to be drastically reduced. This large body of soldier-citizens had fought valiantly against Napoleon. Its officers were mostly commoners, whereas regular army commissions traditionally went to the sons of the aristocracy. All in all, the *Landwehr* was too strongly infected with liberal tendencies to suit the high command.

A noisy controversy arose. The more the monarch and the generals pressed for their plan, the stronger the liberal majority in Parliament opposed it. Constitutionally the House of Deputies had to approve the budget, and without money there was no army reform. To the liberals a stronger army meant a more dictatorial government and greater power for the arrogant officers' caste. Three years of service also allowed more time to indoctrinate the recruits in the habit of unquestioning obedience. This habit would probably stay with them during their lifetime.

Bismarck was, of course, all for the proposed army reform, and William I knew it. They shared the opinion that the military establishment should be free from any control, except by the monarch. Commoners should keep their hands off, for war and everything that went with it were the ancient preserve of the high-born.

On a more practical plane, Bismarck was convinced that a strong army was a necessary tool for Prussia's foreign policy. One did not necessarily have to provoke a shooting war, but the existence of an imposing military force with triggers on the ready could be quite an asset at the diplomatic bargaining table.

Bismarck waited. The King was unable to make up his mind, a weakness he shared with many other royal figures of mediocre ability. Would the troublesome Junker be an asset or a liability in the cabinet? Would he be of help or would he aggravate an already grave situation? The generals pulled in one direction, while even moderate conservatives wanted no part of Bismarck. And Queen Augusta still nurtured her old aversion against him and tried her best to prevent his rise.

The patience of the unemployed diplomat was exhausted. He requested a decision. "Please assign me to a post at once," he wrote, "or else, if Your Majesty cannot find suitable tasks for me, please accept my resignation from government service."

It worked, but not as the writer had hoped. The King still had his doubts, but he did not want to lose a man of such caliber completely. Within forty-eight hours Bismarck had a new appointment —as ambassador to France.

Sensing that his stay in Paris would be of short duration, he did not even bother to move all his belongings there. He had been to the French capital before and had enjoyed the exquisite flavor of its boulevards, its salons and places of entertainment. But now he had no patience for evenings at the cabarets or rides in the Bois de Boulogne. The stifling heat of midsummer hovered like a fiery canopy over the city streets. As was the custom, everybody of means and importance, including government officials and the diplomatic corps, had fled to the beaches or to the cool mountain valleys.

Bismarck still managed to arrange several interviews with Louis Napoleon before the Emperor, too, quit his capital for the country. The French monarch, also known as Napoleon III, liked to chat with the entertaining Prussian, who, in turn, was eager to study the Emperor's mind and intentions. The knowledge gained from such practical psychological observation would be invaluable if ever the two powers should clash.

Eager to escape the dust and dullness of broiling Paris, he found all sorts of excuses for travel. He had barely arrived at his post when he took off for a look at London. Invited to dinner at the British Prime Minister's residence, he practically monopolized the conversation. Astonishment was mirrored in the faces of the other guests as he expounded his ideas with a cocky self-assurance completely alien to Englishmen, who habitually expressed themselves in more subdued tones. In his creaky voice Bismarck declared:

"You ask what I think of German unity? When I take charge of Prussian foreign affairs, I shall declare war on Austria, dissolve the German Confederation, subjugate the middle and smaller states and give Germany national unity under the control of Prussia."

The table company smiled. This man was obviously bluffing. They could not possibly have been familiar with Bismarck's tactics to speak the truth assuming it would be so shocking to his listeners that nobody would believe it.

Only one person recognized this novel technique of disguise by truth. Prime Minister Disraeli advised his guests, "Watch that man. He means every word he says."

Almost immediately after his return from England, Bismarck packed his travel bags again. He felt he needed a longer vacation, though he had hardly put in any time on his new job. He traveled south while Johanna took the children back to her beloved Pomerania.

In Biarritz on the sunny Gulf of Biscay he relaxed and tried to forget that there was a Prussian government, a hesitant King and an obstinate Parliament. Several times a day he plunged into the blue water and swam vigorously for long stretches. Then, floating pleasantly tired on his back, he glanced at the rugged slopes of the Pyrenees, which contrasted darkly and menacingly with the gleaming white of the endless beach. In the evenings he sampled rare French wines at the inns and astounded the vintners with his expert knowledge of all the vintages, whether old or recent, red or white.

The overriding event of this trip was the meeting with Catherine. She was the wife of Prince Orlov, who had been crippled in the Crimean War and was now on vacation from his post as the Russian ambassador to Brussels. Together with their new companion, who towered over them like a legendary giant, the couple spent many hours dining, riding and talking. Often the two men just listened while Cathy, as Bismarck soon called her, played the piano. She was an accomplished musician. Her favorite composer was Beethoven, and his sonatas happened to be about the only music her new acquaintance enjoyed.

He was now forty-seven years old while Cathy was twenty-two. Music, youth and beauty on one side, virile strength and the mysterious aroma of diplomatic secrets on the other, all this under a mellow sun and framed by gorgeous scenery—it was the perfect setting for romance. Bismarck put politics completely out of his mind. The official correspondence forwarded from Paris remained unread and unanswered while he and Cathy swam together in the azure waters of the bay or on horseback visited crumbling castles and lonely lighthouses. The husband had to remain behind because of his infirmities. Whatever he thought about these outings remained locked up in his mind.

Bismarck was young again as every nerve in his body felt the nearness of this lovely creature. The dreaded wielder of the poison pen became a poetic dreamer as he wrote to his wife about the cloudless days at Biarritz:

In front of me the ocean, above me Cathy Orlov at the piano. I write to you by the open window and the flickering oil lamps.

The jingling bells of the carriages in the street accompany the roaring of the sea. In the lighthouse straight ahead of me the red light and the white take turns endlessly. Now the moon has risen and makes the sea glisten, and above me Cathy is playing Beethoven. . . .

Did Johanna have cause for jealousy? If this colorless woman felt uneasy about the idyllic encounter of spring and late autumn, she never indicated it. Her husband's romantic outpourings she answered with homespun requests to see that he did not catch cold in the evenings.

Into the peaceful rose-scented idyll of Biarritz fluttered a telegram. It was from General von Roon and it contained only five words, partly in French and partly in Latin:

Hurry, hurry. Delay is dangerous.

That was all, but it was enough. It was the signal. Suddenly the dream vanished. Bismarck was back in the world of stark, no nonsense reality.

There were tearful good-byes. On their last walk in the foothills of the Pyrenees, Cathy broke a small flowering twig from an olive tree and gave it to her parting friend. For the rest of his life he carried it in his cigar case.

Disappointment awaited him in Berlin. It seemed to have become a regular pattern. Roon had sent the telegram on his own initiative. There was still no official appointment. The political crisis was at the breaking point. As expected, the Chamber of Deputies had voted down the army budget by an overwhelming majority. Young officers passed the word that the time had come for a show of force. The cabinet was in a state of utter confusion, unwilling to abide by the will of the people's representatives, yet also unwilling to go along with an army coup which would send the Parliament packing.

William I was a stranger to the subtleties and compromises of the political arena. All his life he had known only the firm military relationship between superior and subordinate. The one commanded, and the other obeyed. His world was collapsing. How cruel his subjects were that they wanted to deny him his God-given right to lead the kind of army he felt the state needed.

In his gothic summer palace at Babelsberg he sat for long hours brooding in silence. Finally he came to a decision; "If I cannot rule the way my conscience and my sense of duty dictate, I don't want to rule at all."

In the manner of army officers who are denied promotion, he decided to resign. The document of abdication was lying before him on his desk when General von Roon was admitted.

"Your abdication is premature, Your Majesty. We can still save the day."

"How so? My ministers are unwilling to defy Parliament, and I don't want any bloodshed."

"That won't be necessary. The king has the right to dismiss his ministers."

"What good would that do? Others would act just the same way."

"I know one who would not."

"You mean Bismarck? No, he is too dangerous, too unpredictable. Don't call him from Paris, not yet."

"Your Majesty, he is here, waiting in the anteroom."

"What? How dare you act without my orders?" The indignation over this breach of military discipline turned his cheeks purple under the white side-whiskers.

"I am a soldier, Your Majesty. I saw my commander-in-chief in distress and I considered it my duty to act. Please receive Bismarck. He is the man of the hour."

Grudgingly the King gave in. Personally he had never felt quite at ease in the presence of the overbearing Junker, but deep inside he knew that Roon was right.

Bismarck was admitted. The two men talked for hours, first in the private audience hall and then walking slowly along the pathways of the palace garden. The ambassador had carefully rehearsed the stance he would take to overcome his monarch's reluctance. He presented himself as the faithful vassal coming to the aid of his besieged lord as noble vassals had done in times of old.

"How do you propose to get around a hostile Parliament when all my other ministers have failed?"

"My responsibility is only to my sovereign. If I cannot serve Your Majesty with Parliament, I will do it without the legislature. I shall bring victory to royal government and foreclose, once and for all, the supremacy of the assembly."

Suspiciously the ruler eyed the proudly erect figure before him. He sensed that behind this high forehead dwelled a will stronger than his. "Who will make the final decisions, you or I?"

"I will always submit to Your Majesty's orders in the last resort, even if I disagree with them."

This sounded all right, but the King was anxious to get to the point of his most immediate concern.

"Are you willing, then, to push through the reorganization of the army against the will of the majority?"

"I am." The answer was short and clipped. It came without any hesitation.

"It is a dangerous course to take. It may cause a revolution and we may both perish."

"To lose without a fight is cowardice. To perish in a good fight is heroism. But I guarantee that we will not perish."

This was language the old soldier could understand. It touched the concept of honor which had been drilled into him from early childhood. With determined steps he strode to his desk and tore apart the declaration of abdication.

"Herr von Bismarck, I hereby appoint you Presiding Minister of State."

On September 20, 1862, the clouds had finally dispersed. The star was shining brightly in the firmament.

✠ 7 ✠

BAD REVOLVERS

STORMS RAGED ACROSS THE SKY. THEY BROUGHT GRAY CLOUDS
which threatened to blot out the new star before it had barely
begun to glitter.

Bismarck stood before the budget commission of the *Landtag*,
as the lower house of the legislative body was called. The army
expenditures were once more under consideration. Now he had
to face up to the issue which had brought him to the long coveted
top spot in the government.

The reception was decidely hostile. "No more soldiers," said the
dominant liberal faction. "We have too many already." Their mind
was not on new regiments, but on the unification of Germany, which,
they felt, was long overdue. They wanted unification now. Men of
great renown sat among the deputies, none more widely known and
respected than Professor Rudolf Virchow, the world-famous anat-
omist and pathologist.

"All you want," he shouted, "is more bayonets to enslave your
own people. You are doing your best to prevent them from joining
with their German brethren in a nation of free citizens."

Bismarck drew himself up to his full imposing height. The hair
had become thin on his bullet-like skull. Deep circles ringed his
slightly protruding eyes. With dramatic deliberateness he drew
from his cigar case a tiny olive twig, the memento of sweet days
spent in the company of a beautiful young woman.

"I brought this from southern France." The pitch of his voice was even higher than usual. "I intended to offer it to the Progressive Party as a token of peace. I see, however, that the time for such action has not yet arrived."

Slowly he returned the withered stick to the case and the case to his waist pocket while the listeners waited in astonished silence.

"It is true that we can hardly escape complications in Germany, though we do not ask them. Germany does not look to Prussia's liberalism, but to her power—"

Angry outcries interrupted him. "This is typical Junker impudence," shouted Virchow. "Who is Prussia? The people are Prussia. You only represent a bumbling monarch, not the people."

Bismarck leafed contemptuously through his notes. Only after order had been restored did he look up again.

"Prussia must collect her forces and hold them in reserve. . . . The great questions of the time will be decided, not by speeches and resolutions—that was the mistake of 1848—but by *blood and iron.*"

Pandemonium in the meeting room. Deputies jumped to their feet. Some yelled at the top of their voices, others emitted shrill whistles, the supreme sign of disapproval. Slowly the Prime Minister walked out. In the anteroom he again drew out his golden case, this time to select a fat cigar. Only after he could hear no more noise through the open door did he stop smoking and return to the chamber. He was greeted by an angry chorus, "Resign, resign!"

"I am serving at His Majesty's pleasure," he spat at his tormentors, "and I will be the Prime Minister until the King decides otherwise."

It had been a mistake, as he soon realized, to reveal his true intentions so early. The whole *Landtag* was up in arms. The press comments were devastating. The phrase, "blood and iron," remained part of his public image for the rest of his life and beyond. Even his conservative friends shook their heads in bewilderment. Why antagonize one's adversaries so recklessly, so unnecessarily?

Bismarck knew that his position was safe as long as the King was with him. But how long would that be? Old William had only reluctantly accepted him when all other avenues seemed blocked.

Right at the moment he was out of the capital, in the watering place of Baden-Baden, celebrating the Queen's birthday in the circle of the family. He was completely surrounded by the clique of Bismarck's enemies. The Queen never wavered from her animosity. Nor could the Prime Minister expect any sympathy from her son Frederick William, now the crown prince. He was married to Victoria, the oldest daughter of the great English queen of the same name. The crown princely couple sympathized with the liberal cause. In their palace, which had the relaxed atmosphere of a noble British country seat, they surrounded themselves with cultured middle-class intellectuals and artists. No love was lost there for the spur-clanking Prussian gentry, and the name Bismarck was anathema.

William I was so disturbed about the news of his First Minister's "blood and iron" speech that he decided on an immediate return to Berlin. Bismarck knew that his fate was in the balance, but he was not the man to sit and wait for the henchman's axe.

His move to ward off the blow had to be kept completely secret. At the half-finished railroad depot of Jüterborg, an insignificant little town, he awaited the train. Gruffly, in the typical manner of the Prussian official, the stationmaster brushed him off when he asked for the arrival time. Night had come. On the dark, empty platform the Prime Minister sat on an upturned wheelbarrow occasionally jostled about by robust freight handlers.

Finally the shaky oil lantern of the locomotive appeared as a faint yellow dot surrounded by blackness. Bismarck found his master sitting alone in a dimly lit first-class compartment. William looked every year his age. The moment seemed anything but favorable.

"I see well enough how all this will end," sighed the monarch. "On Opera Square, under my window, they will cut off your head—and, a little later, mine."

"And afterward, Sire?"

"Afterward, indeed. Then we shall be dead."

A gloomy beginning, but Bismarck was not easily discouraged. Knowing exactly how to puncture the old warrior's defenses, he intoned his siren song of honor and glory. Had not Frederick the

Great and all the other Hohenzollern ancestors added land and power to their heritage? The Prussian officer's honor code demanded death in fighting rather than retreat. Yes, in France and England kings had died on the scaffold, but theirs was now eternal glory whereas to the detestable regicides stuck the curse of perpetual shame.

The royal heart warmed under the medal-bespangled general's tunic. Forgotten were the dire warnings of wife and son. He could understand that kind of language. When the train pulled into the Berlin station, the waiting dignitaries saw a cheerful King emerge from his compartment closely followed by his confidently smiling Prime Minister.

Publicly Bismarck proclaimed the doctrine of the strong monarchy. What he actually practiced was the domination of a weak monarch by a strong chief minister. The scene in the railroad compartment repeated itself many times, in different settings and with different lines, but always with the same ending. As a staunch monarchist, Bismarck showed remarkably little respect for the crown when he compared his role with that of a skilled horseman who always succeeds in making the restive horse jump according to his will.

As long as he could be sure of the King's grace, the Prime Minister had a free hand. To keep this system effective, he had to see that nothing limited the will of the King whom he controlled.

More stormy *Landtag* sessions followed, and more abuse was heaped on Bismarck's head. But doggedly he pursued his course. Popularity meant nothing to him. When the legislative body continued to vote down the financial requests for army reform, the Prime Minister put the plan into effect anyway. Taxes were collected and expenditures made though no budget had been adopted. Finally the clamor of the *Landtag* became too loud for Bismarck's ears; so he sent it home for the year and ruled by administrative decree. Criticism in newspapers and magazines was muzzled by a vicious censorship. Even elected representatives were punished for their uncomplimentary speeches. Hand-picked servile judges were eager to bend the law to suit the First Minister. After a short period when restrictions had been somewhat relaxed, Prussia was once more a police state of the most oppressive kind.

"Bismarck stands for a regime of the saber at home and war abroad," wrote a liberal deputy. "I regard him as the most dangerous minister for Prussian liberty and well-being."

When he entered upon his high office, Bismarck had, of course, taken an oath to uphold the constitution. Many of his acts were obviously unconstitutional. When confronted with this fact, he cynically replied, "I have sworn to uphold the constitution conscientiously, but what if my conscience tells me not to observe it?"

Why did the people stand for it? Why did not heads roll as the King had so wrongly prophesied?

Prussia was not the right soil for the growth of revolutions. The land was prosperous. Ample revenues flowed into the royal coffers. Long economically backward, the state was now catching up with the general progress of the nineteenth century. In Silesia and in the newly acquired provinces along the Rhine River, coal and iron mines worked full blast to furnish the power for the rising industrial plants. The cities grew rapidly. Swarms of young men and women were streaming in from the villages to work in the new factories and to live in the ugly tenement districts around them.

The *Zollverein* made Prussia the guardian of an expanding common market. In long strings of barges, goods moved on the Rhine and on other rivers from ocean ports to mountain towns. A spider-web of railroads began to cover the state, and the telegraph brought all major points into instant communication. Next to the western Europeans, the Prussians took most eagerly to the miraculously new gadgets of modern technology.

Yet the Industrial Revolution was not followed by any violent political upheaval. Not that everybody was satisfied with the facts of public life. The Progressive Party certainly made itself heard despite police and censorship. Its delegation returned stronger to the *Landtag* after every election. But it was more or less a club of middle-class merchants and lawyers, people who were too well off under the existing system to risk life and limb. True to tradition, the educated minority kept strictly aloof from the unschooled manual workers. This contempt of the simple man who made his living by his hands prevented a stronger and more threatening mass movement. The industrial proletariat was yet weak and unorganized, while the majority of Prussians still tilled the soil for their landlords, a docile and ignorant lot with no loftier goals than a full stomach.

Add to all this a well-drilled army which could be relied upon to move with equal speed against outside enemies or fellow citizens, and a growing number of discharged reservists whose greatest joy in life was to strut in a military parade and display their old uniforms.

In this tranquil setting Bismarck could successfully disregard the feelings of his critics. His personal rudeness increased with age. From subordinates of any rank he required complete submission. Anything short of that was punished by demotion, dismissal or loss of pension. Prussia's foreign envoys were reduced to the function of messenger boys. "My ambassadors," he declared, "must wheel about like soldiers at my command." This was the same Junker who had habitually gone over the heads of his superiors when he was an ambassador.

Not that Bismarck was devoid of human feelings. When his position was not threatened, he could be compassionate. Once he climbed the stairs to the dingy flat of an idealistic rebel. "I have just signed the order for your imprisonment," he told the startled young man. "Tonight the police will come to arrest you. You better get across the border as fast as you can." After the Prime Minister had left, the half-starved foe of the ruling system found a wad of money lying on his bed.

For a time, a most unlikely friendship existed between the chief executive and Ferdinand Lassalle, a talented Jewish lawyer. Bismarck was never bothered by fixed basic principles. Once he had made anti-

Semitic speeches, now his personal financial adviser was a Jew; and for delicate contacts with the French government he used the Paris-based house of Rothschild.

Lassalle, a fiery orator and a clever propagandist, was the founder of the German Socialist Party, the first one of its kind anywhere. Though immensely rich and endowed with a taste for refined luxury, he was on his way to becoming the champion of the industrial workers' class, which, despite the general prosperity, lived in filth and poverty. Every improvement in factory machinery resulted in lower wages and higher unemployment for the workingman.

What greater contrast could be imagined than between the imperious Junker and the Jewish spokesman of the ragged masses. But each respected the other's superior mind. Both were free from narrow dogmatism. In the game of intelligent conversation they were equal partners, and therefore they enjoyed each other's company.

Many a night the slender, hypernervous Lassalle slipped into the crammed building on Wilhelmstrasse which was the Prime Minister's official residence, and the two sat for long hours over brandy and cigars. They discussed their common enemy, the middle-class bourgeoisie. Bismarck attacking from the right and Lassalle from the left, they both zeroed in on the men of wealth and academic knowledge who exploited the workers but wanted a voice in the government which existed largely on their taxes.

Lassalle did not preach revolution, though he called himself a disciple of Karl Marx, another Prussian and now an exile in London. Marx had proclaimed the gospel of the worldwide proletarian revolt against capitalism, but Lassalle sought the good life for the workers by peaceful means. He wanted for the workingman a share in the conduct of state affairs. To this end he advocated universal suffrage. At the time, Prussians voted in three classes, according to the amount of taxes they paid, and each class sent an equal number of deputies to the *Landtag* which, of course, gave the rich an overwhelming advantage over the poor.

"Don't you see, Your Excellency?" Lassalle argued, his finely shaped fingers playing with the silken cord of his monocle. "It would mean the end of the liberal majority which causes you so much grief."

Bismarck had to agree. The ballot of every one of his peasants would weigh as heavily as his own, but he was convinced that Prussian peasants were by nature conservative and always did what they were told by their landlords.

Lassalle spoke of the misery in the workers' districts. "Have you heard of the Silesian weavers? Those simpletons went on a rampage smashing the new machines which were robbing them of their jobs. And the owners promptly reduced the wages of the men they kept. The poor devils don't understand. It's not the machines, it's human greed we must fight."

Again Bismarck had to agree. For him socialism was not the devil's creation as the rich often described it. He could see nothing wrong with workers' cooperatives or with public benefits for the lower classes. In fact, what a boost it would be for the government if it could pose as the true benefactor of the masses. It was not his nature to be mean to the weak. To his peasants at Schönhausen he had always been fair and helpful. If the victims of the Industrial Revolution refrained from revolutionary acts, they should have his sympathy. Large-scale relief of poverty by a kindly, but powerful sovereign would also be a blow to the bourgeois liberals who still subscribed to the outdated *laissez faire* philosophy.

So the odd pair sat and talked. "It was not really a negotiation," Bismarck wrote later, "for I could hardly get in a word edgewise." But he respected his guest, and the admiration was mutual. Lassalle told his friends, "Here is a man. The others are all old women."

The Prime Minister's work in later years clearly reflects Lassalle's lasting influence. But plans for immediate collaboration dissolved due to the sudden death of the irrepressible socialist, a foolish and unnecessary death. A bullet dispatched in a duel over the favors of a young lady prematurely ended the career of the workingman's tribune.

The dictator's days are hardly ever free from trouble. Bismarck had his full share. To the tension caused by the constant alertness against hostile moves and intrigues, his body responded with prolonged upsets. Many a day he had to conduct the affairs of state lying pain-ridden on a couch. But greater dangers lurked about the man who was so hated in Prussia.

One evening he was walking home from the royal palace. After a long, tedious session of the crown council, he was gratefully breathing the fresh air on the tree-lined boulevard Unter den Linden. The sidewalks were crowded; it was the hour when Berliners were taking their customary daily stroll. With light nods he answered the snappy salutes of the promenading officers who recognized him.

Suddenly a young man stepped from behind a tree directly into his path. Without uttering a word, he raised a revolver and fired five shots. They missed except for one which ripped his coat and caused a flesh wound in his side.

Whatever Bismarck was, he was not a coward. Rather than panic, he grabbed the assailant, wrung the weapon from his hand and held him till the police took him away. The fanatic—Ferdinand Cohen-Blind was his name—had felt himself called by providence to rid the world of this tyrant whom so many blamed for everything that was wrong. The same night the prisoner hanged himself in his cell.

Unruffled, Bismarck continued his walk to the official Prime Minister's residence on Wilhelmstrasse. His conviction that God was on his side had been miraculously confirmed. "Don't be alarmed," he told his wife as he slipped into the bedroom to change clothes and have the wound bandaged. "A man tried to shoot me, but all I have is a little scratch."

The narrow private apartment behind the working offices was crowded with dinner guests waiting for the host. Liveried servants were passing drinks to the ladies with feathers and flowers on their elaborate hats and to the gentlemen in uniform or in dark frockcoats which reached to their knees.

Bismarck joined them as if nothing had happened. In his usual manner he regaled them with amusing anecdotes and hilarious, sometimes quite disrespectful impersonations of well-known high-placed figures. No mention was made of the near-fatal encounter on Unter den Linden.

But there had been many eyewitnesses. While the company enjoyed the dinner and the table conversation, the news spread all over the city. The guests were still sitting over coffee and brandy when the royal carriage drove up. The King had come in person to congratulate his chief minister on the happy ending. But many Prussians reacted differently. A certain professor was overheard complaining, "How bad the revolvers in this country are!"

✠ 8 ✠

HOW TO HANDLE A KING

THE QUARRELS WITH PARLIAMENT AND WITH HOMETOWN CRITICS were only a sideshow, as far as Bismarck was concerned. His overriding interest remained the conduct of foreign affairs. In this field he allowed no interference. All decisions relating to the international scene had to remain in the hands of the crown; that meant, practically, in his own hands.

He did not really care deeply about Prussia's domestic needs, nor did he show any profound understanding of them. The resistance he encountered everywhere inside the state dampened his enthusiasm for strong involvement in home affairs. This could wait, he felt. The atmosphere was bound to improve. Just let his critics see how he could secure a more prominent place for Prussia among the nations, and they would be forever silenced.

Prussia was still only a second-rate power with borders which were well-nigh impossible to defend. Her western territories were completely separated from the eastern provinces. Rarely were the voices of her representatives heard when decisions affecting the world at large were made. Everywhere, even in the most advanced countries, abysmal ignorance about Prussian conditions was the rule, and that was true even of the leading foreign statesmen.

Of the four powers which at the moment kept Europe in a state of balance, two traveled a course which made a collision with Prussian ambitions very unlikely. Those were England and Russia. Russian plans called for carrying her flag southward into the Middle Eastern regions which were hundreds of miles away from the Hohenzollern holdings, while England was busy solidifying her overseas empire, which literally stretched around the globe.

That left Austria and France. Neither would stand by idly and watch a single German state rise to worldwide or even continentwide eminence. If Prussia was to grow, those two powers had to be humbled. It was a case of simple, irrefutable logic.

With diabolic cleverness Bismarck set out to plot the triumph of his scarcely twenty million Prussians over the two vastly superior antagonists.

He knew by now that this meant war, not one single war, but several. He was not fond of warfare. The thrust of the bayonet was a crude substitute for the subtle art of diplomacy. Only if the chess game around the conference table was stalemated should the cannon speak. But when that moment arrived, it was to be an hour of Bismarck's own choosing. The army was for him an extended arm of diplomacy. In order to fulfill its function, it had to keep itself in top shape while he saw to it that it never had to face more than a single isolated enemy.

One enemy at a time: this was the only principle which he regarded as sacred. No exception was allowed. Whenever he looked at the map, he experienced something akin to a nightmare. A two-front war had to be avoided at all cost. When in the following century his successors forgot this simple rule, not only Prussia but the whole world was plunged into tragedy.

Bismarck shied from no effort to keep the flanks protected. He made sure of England's neutrality should Prussia go to war, and even stronger were his labors to keep on friendly terms with Russia, for this meant an extremely long frontier which did not have to be defended. How callously he went about securing the Czar's favor became obvious during the Polish insurrection of 1863.

For ages Poland had been an unhappy buffer state wedged in between Russia, Austria and Prussia. During the eighteenth century, its government sank to an unprecedented low of effectiveness. It was corrupt, helpless and completely lacking in popular support. In one of the most unscrupulous examples of naked power politics, her three mighty neighbors got together and decided to divide the unhappy nation among themselves as a housewife may slice up a pie for her family. Though usually quite suspicious of each other, the three found themselves harmoniously united in wiping Poland off the map. Russia received the largest slice, including the capital of Warsaw.

The losers were, of course, the Polish people. The Czarist government behaved especially cruelly toward its new subjects, who, in their desperation, staged a courageous but hopeless rebellion. They received their answer with bullets, with the hangman's rope and with the whips of mounted Cossack troops. The whole civilized world was aghast. Everywhere protest meetings were held and collections taken up for the victims. The loathing of Russian barbarism was general, except in the Prussian foreign office.

For Bismarck humanitarian feelings ended where foreign policy began. "Of the moral powers in the world he has not the slightest notion," commented the historian Heinrich von Treitschke, who was himself an ardent Prussian patriot. The Prime Minister, who always kept also the portfolio of Foreign Minister for himself, concluded a treaty with the Czar allowing the dreaded Cossacks to cross the Prussian border in pursuit of Polish refugees from Russian terror. He had been, up to then, an object of hate only inside Prussia; now his name was uttered with revulsion from ocean to ocean. But for Bismarck it was more important to put Russia in his debt as an insurance against future crises and, at the same time, to issue a warning to the Poles living inside Prussia's own borders.

"Strike the Poles in such a way," he wrote his sister, "that they will despair of their lives. I have every sympathy with their situation, but if we want to exist we cannot do anything else but exterminate them."

As to France and Austria, he worked out a timetable according to which they could be taken on one at a time after they had been put through an incredibly involved diplomatic softening-up process. Austria was first on the list. To cut the Danube monarchy down to size, the whole problem of Germany had to be tackled, and a solution favorable to Prussia promoted. Bismarck realized by now that the general clamor for a single German nation could no longer be neglected. Nationalism was taking on the force of an irresistible avalanche. From the printing presses poured an incessant stream of pan-German propaganda. Chapters of the German National Union, a nationalistic organization with liberal shading, sprang up everywhere, inside and outside of Prussia. Songs about the German fatherland filled the air. All-German congresses were held in this city and that, enthusiastic gatherings of scholars, athletes, glee clubs and firemen who came together from all corners of a yet to be constituted Germany. Everywhere the brotherhood of all Germans was underscored, and the egotism of the petty princes who insisted on holding on to their shaky thrones was condemned.

Italy's unification in 1861 gave German nationalism a mighty shot in the arm. What the Germans so ardently desired, the Italians had just achieved before their eyes under the leadership of Cavour, the astute diplomat, and Garibaldi, the romantic captain of red-shirted revolutionary irregulars.

Bismarck began to swim with the nationalistic tide. In his speeches and pronouncements, the word "Germany" gradually replaced "Prussia." Where he once had spoken derisively of "the German swindle," he now thundered arrogantly: "We Germans fear God and nought else in the world." He did not mind becoming Germany's Cavour, but he saw no need for a German Garibaldi. "In Prussia revolutions are made by kings," he said. He had no use for popular heroes who came not from the palace but from the huts.

If a union of German states was in the cards, it had to be a *kleindeutsche* union, a "little Germany" with the exclusion of Austria. This would leave millions of German-speaking people on the outside, but it would assure Prussian domination of Germany, which was all Bismarck was interested in. This was his real objective as he drew up his master plan with the ruthless determination which had become his trademark.

In the first phase he set about to wreck what was left of the old German Federation and particularly to dig the grave of its Diet in Frankfort, of which Bismarck himself had been a member. Weak and cumbersome as this organization was, it had to go because Austria dominated it. The Habsburg ruler still insisted on some largely ceremonial precedence over the other German princes and expected from them some token of loyalty.

This mystic precedence had to be destroyed. Berlin had to replace Vienna in the hearts of men waiting impatiently for the ascendance of a new Germany. Some occasion had to be found to make so much mischief for Austria that a showdown became inevitable.

Bismarck's opportunity came when, in the summer of 1863, Francis Joseph, the young Austrian emperor, called a conference of all thirty-odd German princes to Frankfort. Rightly he felt that the machinery of the federation needed some drastic overhauling, but wrongly he decided that such a remodeling job was the exclusive business of the various rulers. Here his inbred conservatism came to the fore. The German people were to remain completely unrepresented at this conference.

Francis Joseph wanted very badly to see this meeting succeed. It was exactly on account of this wish that Bismarck set out to wreck it. Even if only moderately successful, such a gathering would add prestige to the house of Habsburg and strengthen the Emperor's role as the foremost German sovereign. This could not be allowed to happen.

Bismarck was determined that his own royal master was not to come to Frankfort. He had to keep the King at home without divulging to him the real reason, and this turned out to be an enormously difficult undertaking. When William I took the cure at an Austrian health resort, Francis Joseph came to invite him personally to the conference. The King accepted; he saw no reason not to. But as the time for the departure to Frankfort approached, Bismarck devised all kinds of ruses to delay it.

All the crowned heads were now assembled in Frankfort, except the ruler of Prussia. Francis Joseph was most anxious to have him present, for without the second most important member, the conference could hardly accomplish anything worthwhile. A fellow king, Johann of Saxony, was sent to fetch William.

The Prussian ruler began to arrange his departure. Now, he felt, his further absence would be considered rude and contrary to all court protocol. Proper behavior had always been a foremost concern of his. For days Bismarck did not budge from his side, as if he were a bodyguard. Only so could he hope to eliminate any outside influence upon the King and fully exert his own. Their arguments were long and hot till they reached a violent climax.

"How can I refuse this invitations from my peers?" William wanted to know. "An emperor delivering it, a king coming in person to repeat it. Impossible."

"But at such a meeting Your Majesty will play second fiddle to the Habsburg Emperor."

"So what? This is the way it has always been. The legitimate princes of Germany deciding her fate under the presidency of the Emperor—it is the right way, the conservative way. Aren't you a conservative too, Herr Prime Minister?"

"Not when it is against the interests of Prussia. If you go to Frankfort you will have to find yourself another prime minister after you get back."

He had shot his biggest bolt. The threat of resignation was his ultimate weapon when everything else failed. A complicated relationship had developed between the two men, the nominal ruler and the actual chief manipulator. The sovereign disliked his cabinet chief, but found him more indispensable with every passing month. Beset with complicated problems which he had never been trained to face, he had to rely on his chief adviser, who always presented him with a perfectly worked out answer. In his limited capacity of understanding, he came to realize more and more that he could not get along without this man. Prussia was growing in strength, and the inner enemy was kept under control. To give Bismarck a free hand always seemed to work out best in the end.

Previously, on the rare occasions when the King proved difficult, the word "resignation" had always sufficed to bring him around.

Now even this technique seemed to break down. William was dead-set on joining his royal cousins at Frankfort. The altercation became more impassioned. Bismarck ran up and down the room like a caged animal from the jungle. A door handle broke off under his powerful grip. The giant broke into tears. His tear ducts always cooperated willingly on such occasions. The scene went on for hours, reminiscent of a violent quarrel between husband and wife.

Finally, after pulling all the registers, Bismarck scored again. He had simply worn the old man down. The end of the drawn-out session found the King lying sobbing on the sofa while the Prime Minister was in such an overwrought state that he grabbed a large glass bowl and smashed it to the parquet floor just to relieve the inner tension.

The King stayed home. A messenger delivered the not entirely false excuse of ill health and frayed nerves to Frankfort. Predictably the meeting of kings ended in a fiasco. No meaningful decisions could be made without the Prussian ruler. Austria lost face, and the German Federation became a laughingstock.

Bismarck had thrown down the challenge. Unless Austria was willing to give up her German position without a struggle, which nobody expected, the next phase would bring the open confrontation of the two leading powers. In his incredibly fertile mind, Bismarck was already pursuing plans to have this confrontation occur on his own terms.

✠ 9 ✠

BLOOD AND IRON

THE CHESS PLAYER PLOTTED HIS MASTER GAME. MANY INVOLVED moves had to be made. The men had to be distributed over the chessboard in just the right position for the final assault on the opponent's chess king.

Why all the complicated preliminaries? Why not just an order to the Prussian armies to invade Austria? No, that would have been too clumsy, too amateurish. Lots of ground had to be prepared first. There was the mood of the population to be considered. After all, the men of the simple people would have to do the fighting and the dying. Potential allies of the enemy had to be discouraged; and what was of extreme importance, William I had to be properly managed so he would underwrite the whole venture.

And the outcome? In any war, one party has to be the loser, and it is hardly ever completely certain which one it will be. Bismarck knew it very well. He knew also that his career, perhaps even his life, was at stake. But the odds were high. It was worth the gamble.

Actually he plotted two wars, one as a preparation for the other. The first one, of short duration and of predictable outcome, was a joint venture of Austria and Prussia against little Denmark. Vienna and Berlin, brothers-in-arms in one fight, enemies in the next—those were the twists and turns of Bismarck's diplomacy.

How ridiculous of Austria to let herself be dragged into such a venture by the sagacious Prussian. The country lay hundreds of miles from the Danish border. There was not possibly anything tangible to gain from the encounter. Bismarck's shrewdness was greatly assisted by the bumbling incompetence of his Austrian counterparts.

The excuse for this preliminary little war was the fate of the two duchies Schleswig and Holstein which lay sandwiched in between Denmark and Prussia. They were not particularly rich prizes of war, except that they controlled the access to the North Sea and to the Baltic Sea. For some time the duchies had been administered by the Danish king though they were not actually part of Denmark. Now King Frederick IV had died without leaving a male heir.

As always in such a situation, the vultures immediately appeared to contest the carcass. A host of contenders put in their claims. Since a large German-speaking population lived in the duchies, nationalistic sentiment throughout Germany ran high in favor of separating Schleswig-Holstein from Danish rule. Somehow the inhabitants were to be integrated into an all-German political framework. But how?

Germany was still only a common name for over thirty independent entities. The details of the various proposals and demands became so complicated that Lord Palmerston, the venerable British statesman, declared, "Only three men in the whole world have ever understood the Schleswig-Holstein question. One was Prince Albert who is dead. The second was a German professor who became mad. I am the third and I have forgotten all about it."

Bismarck had long decided that Prussia could use some, if not all, of the disputed territory. Naively his King objected, "But I don't have any legitimate claim to the duchies."

"Did your illustrious ancestors worry about legitimate claims," countered the Prime Minister, "when they added to the greatness of the kingdom? Did Frederick the Great abstain from bringing glory to Prussia on account of legalities?"

That did it. The word "glory" exerted its usual magnetism. The King's scruples were silenced, and Bismarck had a free hand. To break the deadlock in the confused situation, he persuaded his Austrian counterpart to participate in a joint occupation of the two duchies. Austria and Prussia were to hold them till a permanent solution could be arrived at. There was no doubt what permanent solution Bismarck had in mind. Prussia needed, among other things, good harbors and a secure naval base. But this he did not tell the Austrian chancellor. Nor did he inform him that the newly reorganized Prussian army needed experience in preparation for more important campaigns to come.

Austria swallowed the bait and dispatched some of her regiments to the north. Predictably Denmark tried to defend the duchies, but was no match for the combination of the two mightiest central European powers. Soon she sued for peace.

What next? Now that Austrian and Prussian troops held Schleswig-Holstein, it had to be decided what to do with the spoils of easy victory. Especially Austria did not know where to go from there. But Bismarck had the answer, "Let Austria keep Holstein, and we will keep Schleswig."

This sounded like a good way out of the dilemma if one disregards the fact that Prussia was right next door to its new possession while Austria had no access to Holstein, no knowledge of the local needs and hardly any interest in coping with them.

For thus adding to the Hohenzollern glory, William I made Bismarck a count. This raised him to a status equal with all the higher aristocrats who used to look down their noble noses at the upstart Junker with only a simple *von* in front of his name.

Now it was time to put phase number two of the master plan into operation. On secret orders from Berlin, the Prussian authorities in the newly occupied area did all they could to provoke conflicts with the Austrians next door. The telegraph wires were kept humming with official protests followed by explanations and counterprotests.

With dismay the remainder of Germany looked on. The Federal Diet was still meeting in Frankfort, now completely demoralized by the spectacle of its two largest members going over its head to solve the Schleswig-Holstein question after their own fashion. At this moment of deep frustration, Bismarck launched a bombshell. His ambassador proposed the creation of an all-German parliament based on direct universal male suffrage, just as the late Lassalle would have liked it. This was the same Bismarck who kept his own legislature muzzled and insisted on the privileged status of the titled classes at home.

Everybody realized that, coming from this source, the proposal resulted not from inner conviction, but was a crafty political maneuver. Predictably Austria's objection was violent. Not only did the whole idea offend her conservative principles, but it threatened to relegate her to a minor role in the German Federation, for, under such a plan, only the German-speaking population would be voting. Among all the Austrian subjects of Slavic, Hungarian and Italian nationality they were only a minority.

The needle of irritation had been pushed deep into the Habsburg skin. Angry charges and countercharges were exchanged at the Diet. Driven into a corner, the irritated Austrian delegation finally proposed that all member states should join in armed sanctions against Prussia. Clearly this was a call to war, and it had been issued by the other side. This is exactly what Bismarck had wanted. Prussia could now officially claim to be the injured party.

With this version the Prime Minister came to his King. Only through the fiction of being the victim of aggression could William be persuaded to go along with the new count's plan. Even so it was not easy to get his approval that the military machinery be put into gear. The monarch had grave misgivings about fighting another German power. "Aren't you a German, too?" he asked his Foreign Minister reproachfully. Yes, Bismarck loudly called himself a German now, but the two men did not have the same kind of Germany in mind.

The argument continued for many days. The older he became, the harder it was for the King to make up his mind on important questions, especially when the people closest to him pulled in different directions. The Queen and the crown princely pair were bitterly opposed to any conflict with Austria.

Adroitly Bismarck fed William a steady diet of slanted reports. Little incidents in Schleswig-Holstein were blown up to become examples of gross Austrian arrogance. The words "honor" and "dignity" were sprinkled generously into the discussions. Slowly, but surely, the prospect of war began to fascinate the old soldier who had not seen a battle since, as a boy, he fought against Napoleon. His breast swelled as his thoughts conjured up pictures filled with charging cavalry and with the heroic clash of arms.

The chief minister saw to it that suddenly there was a lot of martial display around Berlin. Picked regiments paraded before the royal palace, and William's eyes clouded with emotion as he listened to the drums and fifes and the rhythmic clip-clop of military boots.

He made his decision. If Prussia's honor demanded a fight, then fight he would.

"I shall draw my sword," the King proclaimed pompously, "at the head of my army, and would rather perish than that Prussia should give way this time."

Bismarck twirled his big mustache with satisfaction. But before he would reluctantly leave the execution of the final phase to the generals, a lot of diplomatic clearing needed to be done to remove possible obstacles in the army's line of march. Neutralities had to be secured and, if possible, allies had to be won. Bismarck did both. In the end there was a two-front war, but it was Austria who had to fight it.

Emperor Napoleon III of France should have been quite concerned about the muscle-flexing of the Prussian neighbor next door. But when Bismarck dropped a few hints that French neutrality might be rewarded by some square miles of land west of the Rhine, the Emperor agreed to keep his sword sheathed.

One of the cardinal rules in Bismarck's type of foreign policy was, "The enemy of my enemy is my friend." This piece of practical wisdom was applied to Italy, the newly united kingdom which straddled the southern frontier of Austria. The Habsburgs still ruled over millions of Italian-speaking subjects whom their now independent brothers wanted to liberate. A deal of mutual assistance was arranged. As soon as Prussia would advance upon the enemy from one direction, Italy was to attack from the other.

The Prime Minister did not forget to stir up trouble inside the

Habsburg empire. Secretly he exchanged words with Hungarian leaders, who smarted under Austrian domination. Could they arrange a little uprising just in time to coincide with the Prussian assault? Here was the curious spectacle of the imperturbable advocate of legitimate authority inciting citizens to rebel against their own government. But that was the government of the enemy.

There was endless coming and going in the narrow, musty corridors on Wilhelmstrasse. Bismarck was always at work, not only in secret meetings but also after hours when he attended dinner parties. In the dinner conversation he let slip seemingly casual remarks, knowing full well that they would immediately be reported to Vienna as significant slips of the tongue. Messages were sent by special couriers disguised as salesmen. Others were dropped in the mail with apparent negligence, but with the full knowledge that they would be intercepted by hostile agents. In addition to all that, a host of professional spies and informers worked overtime.

Finally the preparations were complete. "How does it look from your vantage point?" he asked the top military men, Minister of War von Roon and Chief of Staff Helmut von Moltke.

"We are fully prepared. Everything is ready to go," answered Roon.

"The expedition against the Danes was invaluable as a dress rehearsal," added Moltke. "We corrected some glaring shortcomings."

Moltke had built up the Prussian general staff into a superior brain trust. He was a cool professional for whom war was a matter of efficient performance. The ends which a war was to serve were no concern of his.

"Can we win quickly?" Bismarck wanted to know.

"If things go as planned, it will be within a very few weeks."

Speed was essential. While the Danish adventure had aroused a martial spirit in some Prussians, the great majority still abhorred the thought of fighting against fellow Germans. Antiwar demonstrations were held in the streets, and peace petitions poured into the royal palace. A protracted campaign would intensify the resistance against a war which was commonly regarded as the Prime Minister's private hobby. Long months of fighting might also cause the uneasy neutrals to reexamine their position.

Carefully studying the map of Germany, Bismarck considered the role of the remaining thirty-seven states. Some were so small that they just did not count. Others, especially Bavaria, were definitely in the Austrian camp. Bavaria had old ties with the neighboring Habsburgs. Its people were mainly Catholic, as were the Austrians. A third group had only one desire: to stay on the sidelines while the big boys were having their fight. To them the Count dispatched a terse twenty-four hour ultimatum which he knew to be unacceptable: "Disarm immediately and agree to the exclusion of Austria from the German Federation."

On June 15, 1866, Bismarck was giving a dinner party at his official residence. His French chef was inimitable, and the champagne of his cellar the best in Berlin. Most guests had departed exhilarated by the pleasant evening. Johanna, easily tired by the unwelcome chores of the hostess, was already in her bedroom.

The night was warm and mellow. In thoughtful conversation the Prime Minister was walking in the garden at the side of the British ambassador. Looking at the full moon he pulled a heavy gold watch from his pocket. The clocks on the church towers struck midnight.

"At this moment," he told his startled guest, "our troops are marching into Saxony, Hanover and Hesse." These German states were paying the price for wanting to stay out of the fight.

"A dangerous undertaking," remarked the Englishman. "I hope there will be a minimum of suffering."

"I hardly think so. This struggle will be bitter. If we are beaten I shall not return here. One can only die once, and if one is vanquished it is better to die."

Next morning he exchanged his diplomat's frock for the uniform of a Prussian reserve officer. In the meantime, he had been promoted to major. With some difficulty he buttoned the blue tunic over his protruding midriff. High boots, a spiked helmet and a heavy saber, decorative but useless, completed the uncomfortable outfit.

Then he was off to war. From now on it was the show of the

generals, as he knew only too well. But he had to be close at hand to keep an eye on their doings and mainly not to lose sight of the King who had, of course, refused to stay home. Now almost seventy years old, William was not about to forgo the thrill of sniffing real gunpowder.

The investment in more soldiers, better weapons and ample railroad tracks was paying off. Within three weeks, a speed never before reached, the army was mobilized. With the precision drilled into them day after day, the soldiers executed the commands.

Three long columns moved through the passes of the mountain range which marked the border between Prussia and the Austrian province of Bohemia, today part of Czechoslovakia. The Austrians were slow in mobilizing, but their southern armies had just inflicted a stinging defeat on the Italians. This was Italy's reward for having fulfilled her part of the bargain with Bismarck.

The Prussian armies pushed forward in forced marches. Battle had to be joined before Austrian reinforcements could be brought up from the Italian front. General Benedek commanded the forces under the black-and-yellow Habsburg banner. He had been appointed at the last moment and knew nothing of the terrain. The frightened Viennese government had already chosen a scapegoat.

The morning of decision was here. As the Prussian infantry advanced near the town of Königgrätz, it was met by a devastating artillery barrage, which tore big holes in its ranks. The blue-clad reserves fell back in confusion. The regulars in their green uniforms wavered.

Again the trumpets blared out the signal to attack. Again advance and retreat. No progress was made. Only the heaps of the dead had grown, the screams of the wounded were louder.

Things were not going well. A Prussian army corps which was to have attacked the Austrian flank was nowhere in sight. The earth seemed to have swallowed it. In the meantime, the troops in the field were greatly outnumbered by the enemy.

The missing army corps was under the command of Crown Prince Frederick William. He had staunchly opposed the war. But once the decision was made, he reported for military duty in true Prussian tradition. His corps was given the task to first secure the valuable province of Silesia from possible enemy attack and then to rush to the assistance of the main force.

Mounted on a black horse, King William watched from the bare crown of a hill. By his side, Bismarck, wrapped in a gray cloak, sat on a huge chestnut mare. In the rising mist the big man on the big horse looked like a single mythical creature. They were surrounded by an array of generals. Moltke had just joined them, coming from his Berlin headquarters.

Liaison officers rode up covered with dust and some with blood. They reported and galloped off again with their orders. Bismarck sat rigid as a statue. Moltke nervously fussed with a red handkerchief. From a pocket the Prime Minister drew his golden case and offered the Chief of Staff a cigar. It was refused.

Shells exploded close by. Bismarck urged the King to move out of danger. Fascinated by the sight of battle, the monarch waved him off. He had forgotten that his First Minister was a very determined man. With astonishment he watched Bismarck give the royal horse a hefty kick in the flank with the point of his boot. Pretending not to have seen, William retreated to a safer vantage point.

Now that his sovereign was out of immediate danger, the Prime Minister again turned his attention to the stalemated battle. His protruding eyes scanned the horizon. Suddenly he pushed back his helmet and raised the powerful spyglass which had rested on the pommel of the saddle. There was something in the distance that had not been there before. At first it looked like a row of trees, but it was moving. "The Crown Prince," he shouted.

Once more the trumpets sounded, and the Prussian columns moved forward to meet the foe head-on. At the same time, Frederick William's force tore into the Austrian flank. With deadly effectiveness his soldiers used their new breech-loading needle guns which could fire at four times the rate of the Austrian muzzle-loaders. In terror the enemy gave ground and was soon in disorderly flight. In a matter of four hours it was all over.

"Is the battle won?" asked the exhausted King, who could barely hold himself in the saddle.

"Not the battle," replied Moltke. "The war is won. The road to Vienna lies open before Your Majesty."

In the evening the King and his entourage rode slowly across the battlefield. There had been no time to clear away the heaps of grotesquely mutilated corpses. Many had already been stripped of weapons and clothing by scavengers. "If I think that one day my son Herbert might lie here like this, it makes me sick," said Bismarck. Did he consider that every lifeless soldier on this field was somebody's son? These infantrymen had died, not to protect their threatened homes, but because a brilliant brain lacking in charity had worked out a complicated scheme for the aggrandizement of a dynasty.

That night he slept on a pile of torn cushions from an abandoned carriage. No better quarters could be found. But what did it matter? Robert Keudell, his young aide, told him, "Now you are a great man, Your Excellency. But if the Crown Prince had arrived too late, you'd be an out-and-out scoundrel."

The gamble had paid off. The Battle of Königgrätz, also called the Battle of Sadowa from the name of another town nearby, rates as one of the decisive events in modern history.

Bismarck was the man of the day, and a grateful King pinned a few more medals on his chest. But the project was by no means completed. The most difficult part still lay ahead for Count Otto. Now his unique talent displayed itself in its fullest measure. The warmonger gave way to the statesman. To show restraint in victory is as rare as it is difficult. This is where Napoleon had failed; it has been the undoing of conquerors before and after Königgrätz.

The generals were itching to pursue the fleeing enemy, to dismember the country, to burn and to punish. Loot had always been the powerful lure of the professional soldier. Even the King was captivated by their visions of triumphal marches through Austrian lands. Once aghast at the thought of opposing his Habsburg cousin on the battlefield, he saw himself now in the pose of the gallant victor planting his foot on the prostrate form of the enemy. Yes, by all means, he wanted his grand entry into vanquished Vienna.

Bismarck alone objected. "It is not for us to hold judgment," he told William and his military advisers, "but to make German policy. For the rest, Austria's struggle for existence against Prussia is no more culpable than our own struggle against Austria." The generals were told that Austria was not guilty, just unlucky. It was not what they had wanted to hear.

It turned out to be the hardest struggle of his life. This time the arguments, the sobbing and the shouting lasted for three full days. Several times a day Bismarck threatened with his resignation. In between, he smashed glass and crockery. At one point he seemed to be throwing himself out of the window to the courtyard four stories below.

Only by straining everybody's nerves, including his own, to the breaking point did Bismarck finally win his point. In the Peace of Prague, Austria kept all her territory. Of course, her voice in German affairs was completely silenced, but with her vast possessions in eastern and southeastern Europe she still remained a formidable power. A disarmed enemy was turned into a grateful friend and a valuable future ally. Bismarck had given the most perfect example of his idea that politics is "the art of the possible."

The military clique was deeply disappointed. From then on the relations between the officers' clubs and the Foreign Ministry remained strained. Bismarck did not disguise his contempt for the stiff-necked military mind, while the generals vowed that never again would they let the man in Wilhelmstrasse snatch the sweet fruits of victory from their hands.

But everybody, from king to private, had to acknowledge that, even without Austrian loot, Prussia emerged from the Seven Weeks' War (as the history books soon called it) with some very impressive gains. Hardly a murmur was raised anywhere when Schleswig and Holstein were now quietly incorporated into the Hohenzollern kingdom. The same fate befell a number of other German states which had not sided with it in the conflict. The newly added population amounted to four and a half million. No more gap existed between the eastern and the western holdings. Prussia was now one single compact mass of land.

What was left of the independent German states had received a most impressive lesson. No doubt remained as to which was the leading state, just as there was no question anymore as to who was the leading personality across the width and breadth of the German world.

The capital was decked out in banners and bunting to welcome the returning army. A jubilant mood had turned the prosaic city into a place rocketing with unrestrained merriment. The cheering crowds stood densely packed as the troops marched with precision through the Brandenburg Gate. Flowers descended from windows like multi-colored rain. Flanked by cavalry with capes flying and carbines slung over shoulders, the royal carriage passed by under the hefty cheers of young and old. But the most thunderous ovations were showered upon the man who rode behind the carriage on a huge chestnut mare. Somebody had draped a garland of flowers over his gleaming white dress uniform. Bismarck was flanked by the short and stout Minister of War and the tall, gaunt Chief of Staff. Forgotten were the days when Berliners had thrown stones at him and regretted that an assassin's bullet had gone astray on the same Unter den Linden which now could hardly hold the masses come to hail him.

The rumbling of the drums and the shrill of the fifes had buried the longing for political liberty. Liberals and conservatives alike fell all over themselves to acclaim the man whom they had so bitterly abused only a short time before. A grateful *Landtag* hastened to retroactively approve all the military expenditures which Bismarck had made in disregard of the written constitution. The man of "blood and iron" was now a living legend, an invincible warrior, a symbol of glory and pride.

✠ 10 ✠

IRON CHANCELLOR

WITH GIANT STEPS THE COUNT MARCHED THROUGH THE FOREST, swinging his heavy walking cane. Half his face was shadowed by the broad brim of his shapeless felt hat. The long woolen cape brushed against wild blackberry vines which crept across the path. Two enormous dogs followed, busily sniffing, on the master's heels. Falling farther and farther behind, two privy councilors attached to the Foreign Ministry tried to keep up the pace. Groaning and wheezing they stumbled along, across boulders and fallen trees.

One of them pulled his silver pocket watch. Hopefully he called, "It is nearly dinnertime, Your Excellency. The Countess will be upset if we don't return in time."

They had just emerged in a clearing dotted with blue and red wildflowers. A small stream blocked their way, but there was a footbridge, gray and smooth with age.

"See that knoll on the other side?" Bismarck asked the luckless councilor. "We must climb it first. It promises a good view of all Varzin. The dinner will wait."

Varzin was an estate of 20,000 acres in the Pomeranian backlands. In a rare moment of agreement, the King had proposed and the *Landtag* had ordered a gift of 400,000 taler (about $100,000) to be paid to the man who had humbled the Habsburgs. This was the purchase price for Varzin. As soon as papers of the transaction had been signed, Bismarck had taken off on the five-hour train ride, followed by forty tortured miles in a rattling horse-drawn *landau*. He longed to escape the smell of ink and dust which hovered eternally over the cheerless rooms in Wilhelmstrasse.

His nerves were shattered. Pains and aches raked the huge body after the last months of mental concentration, of pretending and outguessing.

Even in the air sweetened by the tangy scent of the Pomeranian forest, he had passed weeks in sleeplessness and nervous depression. But now he felt better. Four to six hours a day were spent in the saddle or on foot inspecting his beloved groves of oak, beech and pine. Individual trees became his personal friends, and he tried to hide from the forester the fact that some were ailing or overaged to save them from the axe. "When I die," he remarked once to a startled guest, "I want to be hung up in the trees as some tribes of American Indians were accustomed to do."

Financial worries were a thing of the past. He was now one of the wealthiest landlords in the state. Never again would he be embarrassed by the lack of ready cash. He had a lumber mill and a paper factory built to utilize the vast timber resources, and merchants who coveted his good will were only too eager to buy from the powerful statesman.

Again and again he quit his cheerless official residence for lengthening stays at Varzin. Once he did not return to Berlin for five months. He lived in the old manor house which was an ugly monster with a mammoth fireplace. The rooms had crooked floors and ceilings. The roofs were steep and the furniture dark with age. But Bismarck, whose taste was anything but artistic, liked them as long as they were large. Everything around him had to be of outsize proportions, including the dogs.

In his own way he was still a devoted husband and father, taking for granted the subservience of his family. Marie was married to a Count Kuno von Rantzau. The sons had their lives all mapped out for them by their illustrious father. They were destined for government service, but at present they were doing their military duties, both as common soldiers. The Prime Minister had refused any privileged treatment for them.

Johanna von Bismarck was happiest when she could stay with her husband at Varzin. There she saw more of him than she might ever hope to in Berlin. The plain woman fussed over his comfort all day, though her own health became more delicate with every passing year. Public affairs disgusted her more than ever, and it was with a large dose of wishful thinking that she told visitors, "A turnip interests him more than your whole politics."

Right after Königgrätz the Count sounded as if there were some truth in this statement. "For me," he declared, "the best would be to take my leave now. I could do it with the knowledge of having been of some use to the country. Whether I can still accomplish what is left to be done, I don't know."

But he could fool nobody who knew him well. Politics was his world. Without it he felt naked and useless. Daily the courier arrived from Berlin with the big pouch full of state papers, and the regular mail added stacks of letters and newspapers. Then he closeted himself with his two aides in the private study, reading, dictating and penciling marginal comments on the documents. Often he worked through the night and then slept heavily till noon. Through the stream of memoranda which flowed back into the capital, he kept the state organism under his personal control.

Otto von Bismarck was the great man of the day. Legend had begun to surround his image and paint him as superhuman and incapable of failure. Journalists and scholars beat a path to his door, and they came away impressed by his charm and wit. Many voiced surprise at the frankness with which he discussed even the most delicate matters of state. Of course, they failed to realize that his indiscretions were often calculated.

Far less charmed by the treatment they received from him were his colleagues and subordinates. When working with them he blew off steam after playing roles and putting on forced smiles for so long.

He drove his staff relentlessly and lashed the frightened bureaucrats with acid scorn. Patience with fools and blunderers was never one of his virtues.

The Hohenzollern kingdom now possessed an international status undreamed of only a short while ago. But this was only the beginning. Bismarck had upset the old European balance of power; now it was up to him to exploit the new opportunities. Prussia was still hemmed in on all sides. She had to dominate the situation; otherwise she could easily be squashed by a hostile combination of neighbors.

But first the Prime Minister turned his attention to the home base which needed to be strengthened. He was one of the first statesmen to recognize the possibilities of mass communication, but this recognition did not result from any respect of the public. "Nobody despises public opinion as I do," he asserted disdainfully. Yet he used the press extensively to create the right response to his actions, to embarrass opponents by planted disclosures and to launch trial balloons. Exact timing was a skill he displayed in unmatched perfection.

Always the unashamed pragmatist, he found that he could use parliamentary support to put pressure on his King, just as he once used the royal power to browbeat the *Landtag*. To their dismay, his old Junker cronies saw him now flirting with the liberals. His political enemy for many years, the Progressive Party, had split, and the more moderate splinter, calling itself the National Liberal Party, gave him enthusiastic support. On him rested now all its hopes for a speedy unification of all Germans. The conservative block had also sustained a break, and the so-called Free Conservatives had joined the Prime Minister's camp. He could now count on a comfortable majority for all issues he considered important.

With the *Landtag* a willing tool in his hand, he proceeded to the next step in his well-planned quest of making himself the master of all Germany. He created the North German Federation, consisting of Prussia and all the German states north of the Main River which she had not already swallowed up in the wake of the Seven Weeks' War.

Outwardly this was a miniature version of the old German Federation which Bismarck had personally dealt the death blow. But what it lacked in size, it more than made up in strength.

In an almost superhuman spurt of energy, Bismarck singlehandedly wrote the constitution of the new federation. Some features were clearly modeled after the United States, the only sizable federal government then in existence. But there was very little of the American spirit in the document.

The outward similarity lay in the composition of the *Reichstag*, the lower house of the federal Parliament. Like our House of Representatives, it was to be elected through universal suffrage. As in the United States, the constitution also provided for a single system of currency, for one set of import duties and a unified code of laws. But from there on the intent of the paper became distinctly unAmerican.

The various princes kept their thrones and retained, to a large extent, a free hand in domestic affairs. Their personal representatives made up the upper house, the *Bundesrat,* which occupied a position similar to the old Federal Diet in Frankfort. Much more significant was the overpowering position of one state, Prussia. Nothing like this ever existed in the American Union. It made the federation a compact between a lion and a herd of sheep or, as an observer impolitely expressed it, between "a dog and its fleas."

This is what Bismarck had in mind when he called himself a German. The federation did not elect its president; the king of Prussia automatically assumed this position. Prussians dominated both houses of Parliament. In the *Bundesrat* they had 17 votes out of 24. The *Reichstag* consisted of 297 members, 236 of whom were Prussians.

The key feature was that the conduct of military and foreign affairs remained exclusively in the hands of the president. In other words, it was a federation run by a dictator. This dictatorial power was officially vested in the Hohenzollern monarch; practically it was exercised by Bismarck.

Retaining his offices as Prussian Prime Minister and Minister of Foreign Affairs, he vested himself now, in addition, with the only federal office his constitution provided. He became the single Minister of the North German Federation, soon to be called the Chancellor. It is as the "Iron Chancellor" that he became a historical personality ranking with the great of all times.

The Chancellor was responsible only to the King-President, whom he could handle with such finesse. Under its new black-white-red flag, the North German Federation became the instrument on which he could practice his superb musicianship as he had done on the smaller Prussian model before. Immediately he saw to it that tough Prussian drill sergeants took the raw recruits from every corner of Northern Germany under their wings. All the twenty-two member states immediately felt the whip of Prussian no-nonsense discipline.

A civilian at heart, Bismarck had always loathed the bombastic airs and closed minds of the officers' caste. But he found it prudent to play up the army, the mighty sword of the federation. His civilian dress gathered dust in the wardrobe chest while he took on the habit of appearing before the public in military uniform. Innumerable portraits show the reserve major in his blue tunic with the order of the Iron Cross dangling on his chest and with boots reaching well above the knees. This is how the world came to regard him. There were moments when he even deluded himself with the notion that he liked to be a fighting man. Once he said, "I regret that I was not granted the honor of serving my king only as a soldier." He had his chance when he was young, and it was anything but a notable success.

The military might at the disposal of William I extended far beyond the boundaries of the federation. After the war, the remaining German states to the south—Bavaria, Württemberg and Baden—entered into a secret military alliance with the North. By a shrewd combination of threats and promises, Bismarck forced them to put their soldiers under federal, which meant Prussian, control in case of war. This was in direct violation of an agreement the Chancellor signed afterward with Napoleon III. "It is not a rare event in history," wrote an Austrian statesman, "that treaties are broken. But that a treaty is broken beforehand, that was an innovation reserved to the genius of Bismarck."

Why did he not bring the Southerners into the federation outright? German nationalism, which had reached an unprecedented crest, clamored for it loudly enough. He had his good reasons.

As in America, North and South were more than just geographic distinctions. Customs, traditions, dialects were quite different. Mostly Catholic by faith, the South Germans were easygoing and appreciated beauty much more than their Prussian brethren. Munich, the capital of Bavaria, was a center of art and gaiety, ranking only behind Paris and Vienna. Nobody there wanted to be ordered about by Pomeranian Junkers, least of all the three South German princes who still commanded sizable armed contingents.

But the most compelling reason for leaving the South, for the time being, out of the German fold was France, the suspicious big neighbor. For more than twenty years Napoleon III had been holding forth there. His likeness with the black goatee and the panhandle mustache was displayed on a thousand walls, but much more attractive was the picture of Empress Eugenie, a woman of rare beauty. The two formed a clever, ambitious team, determined to cash in on the magic name of the great predecessor and trying hard to equal his accomplishments. At first Napoleon III spoke with a commanding voice in European affairs, but lately he had been slipping. One of his most painful reverses was the futile attempt to rule by proxy over Mexico. Like so many men who are gifted, but not great, he had overreached himself, forgetting Bismarck's lesson that "politics is the art of the possible."

Now he was a sick man, driven by an overambitious wife and troubled by deep dissatisfaction among the French citizenry.

Bismarck knew the Emperor quite well. They had met in Paris during his days as an ambassador and also at Biarritz where Napoleon tried to regain his lost health. Both were shrewd and cynical, but Bismarck's talents towered high above the Frenchman's, whose painful ailments were robbing him of strength and willpower. His inability to take decisive action was to bring about his downfall.

France had watched Prussia's rise with deep concern. A weak and divided Germany had always been her best protection. Napoleon III considered the South German rulers his special protégés. It was he who had insisted that they stay out of the federation, and Bismarck knew how to wait.

Austria's defeat in 1866 came as a complete surprise to Napoleon. He had counted on a Habsburg victory or at least on a long, destructive war, enabling him to step in as the mediator between his chief competitors. If he could thereby gain some territory as his broker's fee, it would give him a much needed boost in popularity at home.

To assure France's neutrality, Bismarck had once made some vague hints at a special reward. To the French ambassador he had indicated that he would look the other way if Napoleon helped himself to some French-speaking territory, say, for example, Belgium. Diplomats continually engaged in territorial horse-trading as if only trees or cattle existed on such land and not people. Even then the small countries were not more than bite-size prey of the hungry big powers.

After the shooting had stopped, Vincent Benedetti, the French envoy, came to claim the reward. But neither he nor his master was a match for Bismarck's cunning. He strung the Frenchmen along till they realized that all the hints made before the war had been conveniently forgotten.

The Chancellor's mind was made up that an armed conflict with Napoleon was unavoidable if Germany should be united and secure. France would never resign herself voluntarily to a new superpower next door. Certainly the Emperor would lose his throne if he allowed it to happen.

Was Bismarck alone responsible for the Franco-Prussian War? Historians have argued the point long and hard. Undoubtedly he would have avoided the clash of arms if he could have achieved his ends peacefully. It was not his habit to provoke a fight just for the sake of fighting. But it took no particular clairvoyance to realize that

France was not about to commit political suicide. "I never doubted," Bismarck wrote in retrospect, "that victory over France had to precede the unification of Germany."

So he plotted the third war of his career with all the attention to detail that was his trademark. Again the enemy had to be diplomatically isolated. Again she had to be maneuvered into the role of the aggressor. Only so could the Chancellor be sure that the South Germans would actually fight on his side. The mingling of German blood on the battlefield was to provide the insoluble glue of complete unity.

Their location had made Germans and French traditional foes. On both sides superpatriotic propaganda disseminated hate and distrust. Yet, paradoxically, the educated German had always been fond of French culture. Even the Prussian King sprinkled his speech liberally with French phrases. Bismarck himself liked not only the language but many products of France, especially those that were edible or drinkable.

But likes or dislikes were not allowed to interfere with the quest for power. In 1867 he visited the French capital again in the retinue of his King. The crowned heads of the world and their chief assistants descended in droves upon the Seine River where the Paris World Exposition was held. The populace was treated to the spectacles of military parades and magnificent fireworks. Parisians danced in the streets and ogled the passing celebrities. An enormous pleasure park had sprung up on the bare Mars Field, where musical bands from all nations blared continuously to attract visitors to their pavilions.

Bismarck refrained from plunging into the inviting pool of Parisian pleasures. In the afternoons he took long walks on the outskirts of the city in the company of Moltke, the Chief of Staff. Without any show of interest they passed charming châteaux and quaint villages along the way. They were after a different kind of tourist attraction.

"See that hill over there, just behind the village cemetery?" asked Moltke.

"What about it? You think it would do?"

"Most certainly. The slope is gentle enough to drag a cannon up, and the line of vision is undisturbed."

"What about the distance?"

"Just right. The shells would fall into the outer city where the factories stand and where the population is especially dense."

Moltke made a few entries in a little book he carried in his pocket. "Now we have to find a few more points like this."

And they wandered on along the roads which ring the city on the Seine.

✠ 11 ✠

LONG LIVE THE EMPEROR

WAR CAME IN 1870, AND IT CAME ON BISMARCK'S TERMS. THE immediate cause would seem utterly ridiculous to anybody not familiar with the strange ritual of royalty. Kings hold sacred things over which nobody else would lose a minute's sleep.

It all began, not with an event in France or in Prussia, but with a vacancy on the Spanish throne. Once a mighty empire over which the sun never set, Spain was now a corrupt and backward country. Queen Isabella, the last Bourbon ruler, had just been driven out on account of her flagrant lack of honesty and decency. Republics were not yet in style, so the search for a regal successor began. Where does one get a king in a hurry? Of course, he has to be of royal blood. In fact, this is about the only requirement for the job.

After a long search, the Spanish parliament, the *Cortes,* finally settled on Prince Leopold of Hohenzollern, a relative of the Prussian ruler. Since William I was the head of the family, his permission was needed for the candidacy of the young prince. He refused, assuming very correctly that France would not like this at all. To be surrounded by Hohenzollerns to the south and to the east was not a situation Frenchmen would have cherished.

But Bismarck wanted it otherwise. He insisted with his well-proven tactics that the King reverse his decision, and Bismarck, as usual, won. As it turned out, the whole Hohenzollern candidacy had been the Chancellor's idea to begin with. Through bribes and various secret palavers he had put the Spaniards on to it and thereby laid a trap for the hapless Napoleon.

The effect was exactly what the foxy Chancellor had anticipated. Paris reared like a wounded bear. "A Berlin" (On to Berlin), shouted the hysterical masses on the boulevards. The man in Wilhelmstrasse seemed to have his little war all wrapped up.

But even the canniest operator can see his plans circumvented by a slip-up. The unforeseen occurred. Bismarck, feeling that everything was taking its charted course, was relaxing at Varzin, while his ailing King tried to restore his health at the watering resort of Ems. There he was handed a strongly worded protest of the French government. Since he had been against the whole business to begin with, he quickly withdrew his consent to Leopold's candidacy. He wanted peace, or at least he did not want war on such a paltry excuse. The affair seemed settled. Everybody breathed easier, except Bismarck.

Another unforeseen development changed the whole situation once more, an accident of which only a man like the Chancellor could have taken advantage. Badgered by the nationalistic fanatics in the streets of Paris, the French cabinet lost its head. It should have been very satisfied with the turn of events, but no, it had to stir up the simmering brew. Urgent instructions went out to Ambassador Benedetti.

It was a clear morning. The rich lawns were still moist from the nightly dew. Not many strollers were abroad on the flower-fringed promenade of Ems. As was the custom for patients seeking the cure, William I had drunk his mineral water and was now slowly walking through the stately park. To maintain his privacy, he was garbed in civilian clothes. An adjutant kept discreetly a few paces behind the old man.

On one of the benches which were distributed along the path sat the French ambassador. The King had taken a liking to the elegant Frenchman, and so he stopped to exchange a few polite remarks. It turned out that the diplomat was not there by accident. Knowing the monarch's habits, he had lain in waiting.

"I am sorry to disturb your morning walk, Your Majesty. I must deliver a most urgent message from my government concerning the Spanish succession."

William's face darkened. The beautiful morning had been spoiled for him. "This silly Spanish business again? I have already withdrawn my consent. What more do they want?"

"My government insists on an apology and on a promise that you will never in the future permit a Hohenzollern to covet the Spanish throne."

"But this is impertinent. Do they doubt my sincerity? Do they question my honor?"

They argued. They raised their voices till curious early promenaders began to crowd in. In high anger the King signaled his aide, and they walked off leaving the embarrassed Frenchman to himself.

When Benedetti called at the royal residence at a later hour, he was not admitted. William was in a very bad mood. He had hoped to enjoy this little vacation undisturbed, and here they were annoying him with their silly politics. Why wasn't his Chancellor here to take care of such matters? Still irritated, he dictated a dispatch informing Bismarck of the day's events and leaving it up to him to publish the contents if he found it advisable. With that he put the whole event out of his mind, perfectly sure that the disagreeable storm would soon blow over.

This routine message from Ems to Berlin was to go down in history as the crucial "Ems Dispatch."

Berlin was unbearably hot and steamy on that July 13. Bismarck had just returned from Varzin and was having dinner with Roon and Moltke. Gloom lay heavily over the dining room with its tasteless oversize table and chairs. The two military officials, both now old men, hardly touched the food, and even Bismarck's peerless appetite had almost evaporated. "I just sent word to my wife at Varzin not to follow me," he growled. "I'll be back there shortly and this time for good. It is all my fault. I should never have left the King alone in Ems."

Moltke's clean-shaven face was pale and haggard. "All this planning, all the minute preparations—for nothing. I might as well give up, too."

For years the general staff had worked on the war with France. The officers' corps knew every square mile of French territory better than the prospective enemy. Weapons and ammunition were stockpiled in generous quantities. The men in charge were ready for every eventuality, except the change of their unpredictable sovereign's mind.

An orderly brought a long telegram in code which had just arrived from Ems. It was promptly deciphered. Without too much interest Bismarck glanced at it. Suddenly his posture stiffened. The eyes had lost their dullness. He read it over again. Exultantly he turned to his friends. "Perhaps things are not as drab as all that. Wait a bit. I have a job to attend to."

He stepped into the untidy study. Paintings, many of them gifts from crowned heads, were carelessly stacked in the corners. At his desk he pushed away a litter of books, maps and railroad timetables. Before him was the message from his king and a blank sheet of paper. In the dining room his guests looked at each other in uncomprehending silence.

He was back in a short while. "Here, listen to this. I have not added anything, just shortened it from twenty-four to twelve lines and done a bit of rearranging. This will go out immediately to all the papers and to our embassies. The papers must publish extras. The ambassadors must inform the foreign governments without delay."

They all compared the two versions. Now the report sounded as if Benedetti had been extremely rude to the King, and William had brushed him off in fury, refusing to ever receive him again.

The two generals were in a state of ecstasy. As if by command they pushed back their chairs.

"Now it has quite a different ring," said Moltke. "First it sounded like a friendly parley. Now it is like a flourish of trumpets in answer to a challenge."

Bismarck was exultant. "It will have the effect of a red rag on the Gallic bull."

"Our God of old still lives," added Roon. "He will not let us die in disgrace."

Suddenly Moltke looked younger. His usual reserve was gone. He pounded his chest with a lean fist. "If I may but live to lead our armies in such a war. Then right afterward let the devil come and haul away the old carcass."

"Is everything ready?" asked Bismarck.

"Ready and waiting for the call to advance," was the chief's answer.

With a bottle of the choicest champagne they toasted the now inevitable war. It was French champagne.

The news hit the Parisians just as they were celebrating Bastille Day, their national holiday, in the streets. No politician dared stem their fury. Only blood could now wash away the insult to French honor. Benedetti, who had been the involuntary instrument of a tragic fate, put in one more appearance at the Berlin Foreign Office. Gravely he handed Bismarck the declaration of war. The French had taken the first step.

In its early stages the Franco-Prussian War was almost a replay of 1866. With flawless speed nearly one million Germans from north and south answered the call to arms. Everybody knew exactly where to go. Everything the mobilized soldier needed he found in its proper place. With songs on their lips they marched into the territory of the enemy whose mobilization had bogged down in confusion. French soldiers were without ammunition, officers without their men. A hastily appointed top commander was unfamiliar with local conditions.

Before a dumbfounded world could catch its breath, one French army had been thrown back into the fortress of Metz and completely cut off. Another found itself hopelessly surrounded in the town of Sedan and capitulated after brave, but futile resistance. Among the prisoners was Napoleon III. "In one day," wrote Bismarck, "the French lost a hundred thousand men and one emperor."

At the first whiff of gunpowder, the warrior King had taken off for the front with the Chancellor in hot pursuit. Since the Ems episode he was more determined than ever not to let his sovereign out of sight. For almost a year he conducted the affairs of state from requisitioned burghers' houses and from peasants' huts close to the scenes of fighting. He slept little, and often the food was scarce. Yet he seemed to draw on unknown resources of strength.

All the old aches and pains had disappeared as if by magic. After long hours in the saddle, he spent the nights engrossed in paperwork which seems to be the unavoidable by-product of every governmental activity. His staff groaned under the killing pace. Numerous visitors intruded upon the Chancellor's precious time. German princes came who did no fighting, but expected medals for the victories, and also interested foreigners, such as General Sheridan of the United States.

The sun of victory did not illuminate Bismarck's days with bliss. A courier brought to his improvised desk the news that Herbert, who served with a cavalry regiment, had been killed in battle and his brother Bill severely wounded. The father finished dictating an important letter. Then he rode alone into the night, across the ripening fields and the thick hedgerows of northern France. Before his tortured mind was the picture of the silent battlefield at Königgrätz over which he had ridden four years ago.

It turned out that through some communications foul-up the report had been grossly exaggerated. Bill had been thrown from his horse, but was unhurt. Herbert lay bedded on a pallet of straw with a bleeding but simple wound in the thigh. Father and sons exchanged a few proper remarks, their true feelings restrained by military etiquette. Bismarck was impatient to return to his interrupted work. Soon afterward both sons received their permanent release from the army.

There was other trouble, more persistent, and in the long run, more galling. The military attempted to exclude Bismarck completely from the conduct of the war. Though he carried now the more or less honorary rank of general himself, he was not admitted to the councils of strategy. Often he had to depend on the newspapers and on interviews with war correspondents to find out what was going on. The high brass wanted to make sure that he would not spoil their victory as he had done in 1866. Such unaccustomed treatment was hard to take.

Despite the stunning defeat at Sedan, the French fought on. Dismayed by the incompetence in high places, they overthrew Napoleon, who was now held prisoner in an obscure castle. Ignominiously he faded from the scene. A republic was established, the third but not the last in the turbulent course of French history. Paris was in revolt. Bloody civil war compounded the national tragedy.

Having engineered the conflict, Bismarck was now very anxious to end it. But there was no government in France stable enough to be partner to a permanent peace treaty. So the war dragged on. Paris, tormented by strife within, was under siege by the Germans who, in turn, were plagued by *franctireurs,* the grim and desperate French resistance fighters.

Despite their minute planning, the Prussian leaders had not reckoned with a prolonged conflict. They had not envisaged fighting a whole nation in arms, dealing with starving women and children and listening to the cries of outrage coming from compassionate people all over the world.

The Chancellor saw his whole elaborate scheme threatened. What if England or Russia or a combination of them now changed their minds about their intended neutrality? They had been told that Prussia was the attacked party, but now the war could not be excused anymore as a defense of the German fatherland. It was naked invasion of another nation which had long stood before the world as the guardian of culture and progress. His old ailments returned. Secretaries and servants had to put up with his fits of irritation. At times his impatience made him lose his good sense to an alarming degree.

Once when he was in such an irrational mood, he suggested that the troops should fire on starving civilians who wandered too close to the German positions in search of food scraps. When someone remarked that the soldiers might refuse to do this, he answered angrily, "Then you'll have to shoot the soldiers for disobedience." And when supplies were running low, he callously recommended, "Take no more prisoners of war because corpses need no shelter or food."

All this did not increase his popularity, but it was nothing compared to the revulsion that greeted his statement that now was the time for a concentrated artillery bombardment of Paris to bring about a quick end of hostilities. The world was aghast at the prospect of seeing the "Mecca of civilization" in smoldering ruins. Bismarck only scoffed at these expressions of the "humanitarian swindle," blaming them mainly on the Crown Princess and her British connections.

Fortunately the generals continued to ignore his advice. A few scattered shells fell on the capital, but a sustained bombardment was rejected as of scant military value.

While Paris starved, the palace of Versailles, some fifteen miles away, became the temporary headquarters of the North German Federation. The splendid edifice erected to proclaim the glory of Louis XIV of France, now housed the German princes, the high command and countless hangers-on.

Bismarck disdained the ornate, but uncomfortable palace and lodged himself in a simple yellow townhouse nearby. One cluttered room served as his office and sleeping quarters while in the only other one he received visitors. Prussian militiamen with long pipes hanging over their beards stood guard at the entrance. In the evening the chief assembled his staff for dinner which was eaten from tin dishes. The supply of wine was good. They were, after all, in the wine center of the world. Empty bottles with candles stuck into their necks substituted for chandeliers. On a piano, long out of tune, Keudell, the faithful aide and confidant, played Beethoven from memory.

Though the Chancellor ran up against a stone wall on points of military strategy, he was by no means reduced to idleness. Some unfinished business remained which only he could attend to. It was the task of founding the German Empire. This is what the war was to have been all about.

The southern states still had to be incorporated into the German framework. Napoleon, the main obstacle to the union, was a tragic has-been. The world wondered at the indomitable display of Prussian military might, and the sight was not lost on the three princes still outside the federation. Soldiers from north and south had fought and died side by side. German national pride was at its jubilant climax. This was the moment. It might never come again.

Still the job was fraught with complications. The three rulers, especially the King of Bavaria, were hard bargainers. Bismarck had to deploy all his resources of cajolery, deception and threat to bring them around. His contempt of princes was only equaled by his bitterness toward generals.

One by one, the Kings of Bavaria, Württemberg and Baden swallowed the angler's bait. Large sums of money changed hands in secrecy. Princes were usually in debt, and so were their influential advisers. Each ruler was told that the others had already joined, that he better get on the bandwagon or face the combined hostility of the German nation. It worked.

The enlarged federation was to be called the German Empire to suggest a historical connection with the medieval empire, which, at times, had extended from the Spanish coast to the steppes of Hungary. All that was needed now was an emperor, and naturally there was only one candidate for this position.

If Bismarck had hoped that his master would eagerly accept the promotion from king to emperor he was sadly mistaken. William, in his simple and stubborn way of reasoning, felt that King of Prussia was the proudest title any mortal could hope to hold. He was not about to add to it a nebulous office which, in the past, had often carried little or no real power.

Yet Bismarck was convinced that the title was of prime importance. It symbolized unity. While the Kings of Bavaria and Württemberg might balk at accepting the King of Prussia as their superior, it would not look humiliating to bow to the Emperor of Germany.

To the last moment the weary old man resisted Bismarck's tricks and blandishments. He gave way only when the Chancellor pressured the other princes to literally beg him. Still he had strong misgivings and was extremely vexed at his persistent Prime Minister.

As a dramatic symbol of German power, the final act of the play was staged, not on German soil, but deep in enemy territory, on the spot of France's proudest memories. On January 18, 1871, a splendid company assembled in the Hall of Mirrors, the most sumptuous part of the palace of Versailles. The seventeen full-length arched windows on one side were matched by an equal number of mirrors on the opposite side. This gave the 240-foot-long room the illusion of being many times wider than it actually was. The crystal chandeliers were ablaze to dispell the wintry semidarkness and to illuminate the marble and gold along the damask walls.

The highly polished parquet floor resounded to the unaccustomed tramp of Prussian boots as the standards of some sixty regiments were carried to the dais. Before the half-circle of flags, William I, pale and his hands slightly shaking, took his place surrounded by his fellow princes. Men of high military rank filled the whole length of the enormous hall. No civilians could be seen, no representatives of the German people.

Heels clicked to attention as a preacher invoked divine guidance. The King of Prussia welcomed the assembly in a faltering, barely audible voice. Then Bismarck, standing directly in front of the King, unrolled a parchment scroll embossed with a large red seal. His voice was cool and businesslike as he read the proclamation:

> We, William by the grace of God, King of Prussia, and after the German princes and free cities have unanimously appealed to us to renew the imperial dignity . . . therefore inform you that we regard it as our duty to assume the German imperial title.

The Prince of Baden raised his arm and shouted, "Long live Emperor William." With three rousing cheers the titled and bemedaled throng responded. The German nation was a reality.

The new Emperor, now seventy-three years old, stepped from the dais and shook hands with all the generals who crowded around to congratulate him. He passed right by Bismarck, who stood there with outstretched hand, completely ignoring him. The slight was plain to everybody present. Like a sulking child, the new Emperor took his little revenge on the man who alone was responsible for this triumphant occasion.

Not a muscle moved in the Chancellor's impassive face. But back in his quarters, the suppressed resentment erupted in a spasm of sobs. Then he sat down and wrote his wife:

> Forgive me for not having written to you for so long, but this imperial childbirth was an extremely difficult business. Kings at such times have strange cravings before they give to the world that which they cannot retain with them any longer. . . .

✠ 12 ✠

THE AGE OF BISMARCK

AGAIN THE ARMY ENTERED THE CITY TRIUMPHANTLY, AS IT HAD five years earlier. But it was a different city decked out not in jubilation, but in mourning.

Through the streets of Paris marched the German columns. Officers, sabers drawn and balanced against their shoulders, danced their horses on the pavement. Behind them strode the tight ranks in precision step. Drums beat the time in an endless staccato. The rifles and bayonets of the infantry, the short carbines of the cavalry and the caissons of the artillery, all wore the high polish required for the parade.

It was May, and the trees along the broad Champs Élysées were in bloom. Row upon row, the Prussians and the Bavarians, the Hessians and the Saxons wheeled into the splendid parkway. The fifes, the trumpets and the *glockenspiel* gave out with martial music that was punctuated by the clop-clop of horses' hoofs and the command shouts of the officers.

Absent were the cheering throngs, the flowers, the proud citizens who had turned Berlin into a city of rejoicing in 1866.

The victors marched arrogantly through vanquished Paris, but the sidewalks were empty. From behind shuttered windows the Parisians stared at the triumphant Teutons. Only a scattering of the most curious stood on the corners, sullen and silent. Fists were clenched, but they remained hidden in coat pockets. Some men cried.

The majestic Arch of Triumph on the wide circular Place d'Étoile had been erected by Napoleon to glorify France's greatest days. It was a revered shrine to millions of her sons. In the shadow of the monument, the lead group fell out and took position according to rank. They were all on horseback, the Chief of Staff, the commanding generals and also the Chancellor in his blue tunic with yellow facings and white cap.

While a military band thundered one marching tune after another, the troops passed by in review, flags lowered and heads turned sideways in salute. They marched on to bivouac on the Place de la Concorde where once the guillotine had done its gruesome work.

Bismarck did not follow them. When the last regiment had left the reviewing group behind, he turned his horse and slowly rode toward the edge of town. He wanted to be alone. Doubts assailed him. Gloom and forebodings of tragedy displaced the pride of fulfillment which should have possessed him on that day.

Peace had come at last, but it was not the peace of wise moderation which had been granted the Austrians. This time the generals had their way. They wanted to taste the full sweetness of victory. The visible humiliation of the defeated symbolized by the triumphal march through the streets of Paris was one of the points they had insisted on.

Tired and dispirited, the Chancellor realized that there was no use struggling against the tide. The generals might as well have their fun. He knew the French were so deeply wounded in their pride that no amicable gesture would reconcile them. From now on only one passion would flame in their hearts: revenge.

Far more important than the childish military display were other provisions in the Treaty of Frankfort, which concluded the fateful Franco-Prussian War. A financial penalty of five billion francs (about one billion dollars) was levied against France. It was an old rule of the game that the loser paid everybody's expenses, but never before had the greed of the victors exacted such a staggering price.

By far the most searing wound was the territorial clause of the treaty. The new French Republic lost two of its richest provinces, Alsace and Lorraine. Though the two million inhabitants spoke mostly a German dialect, especially around Strasbourg, the main Alsatian city, they were perfectly content to be French citizens as they had been for two hundred years. Yet nobody bothered to consult them about their feelings.

Bismarck had grave misgivings about the annexation. "I just don't like having so many Frenchmen in the house who don't want to be there," he said. On this point he found himself in agreement with Karl Marx, the founder of communism, who correctly predicted that the loss of Alsace-Lorraine would make France an implacable enemy and drive her into the arms of any power hostile to Germany.

But the military experts had insisted that the provinces were absolutely necessary for the future defense of Germany. Very tempting also were the vast iron deposits in Lorraine which would soon play a vital role in propelling the wheels of Germany industry.

The land grab was simply an act of force. But not content with this brutal fact of life, some nationalistic historians tried, by twisting a few facts here and there, to prove that Alsace and Lorraine were really lost children of the German fatherland. Bismarck himself was not impressed by such arguments. Ever the champion of *realpolitik,* he dismissed all those high-sounding arguments as "professors' ideas." In his vocabulary the term "professor" was an insult.

Thus ended the last of the three wars which the Iron Chancellor had painstakingly planned and majestically won. Now he directed the most powerful nation on the continent, as he had intended from the beginning of his career. For the next twenty years, he was to remain Germany's ruler in all but name. Far and wide he was hailed as the leading statesman of the century. It became quite the thing to compare him with Napoleon. The American John Motley, who had met Bismarck when they were students in Göttingen and had remained his lifelong friend, called him "the greatest living man and one of the greatest historical characters that ever lived." So massive was his impact on the world that scholars soon began to refer to the seventies and eighties of the last century as the Age of Bismarck. Such a tribute has been bestowed on only a very few personalities of the past.

If the whole world felt that way about Bismarck, it can easily be understood that inside Germany neither friend nor foe disputed the massiveness of the shadow he cast on the national scene. Hardly any opposition was raised as he now proceeded to organize the new empire. The cloak of government was cut to fit his own measurements. Actually the new empire was a mere extension of the North German Federation which, in turn, had basically been an enlarged Prussia. Prussian cement had been mixed first with a smaller, then with a bigger portion of German sand till a giant solid structure emerged.

Germany was now a federation of monarchies. Enlarged versions of the *Reichstag* and the *Bundesrat* were retained. The King of Bavaria and all the lesser princelings kept their crowns and their fancy palaces, and the Emperor found to his immense relief that he was still King of Prussia. With the passing of time his aversion to the imperial title evaporated. He came to like it and to wear the emperor's mantle with immense pride.

As William began to enjoy being Emperor, his grudge against Bismarck changed to gratitude, and he showered the architect of the empire with rare honors. There were more stars and crosses for his tunic and also a new title. He was elevated to the rank of an honorary prince, which meant that callers now had to address him as, "Your Serene Highness." He reacted to all these rewards with the remark, "I would have preferred a horse or a barrel of good Rhenish wine." Who can be certain whether this indifference was real or only pretended?

A further reward by his generous sovereign was the ducal estate of *Friedrichsruh* (Frederick's Rest) near Hamburg. Now he had two retreats, these new thirty thousand acres and Varzin. He alternated between them during his steadily lengthening periods of absence from the capital.

Though hastily assembled, the machinery of the German Empire functioned to perfection. At the controls sat the Imperial Chancellor, a solitary crusty figure with untold admirers and very few friends. Nobody but the Emperor could dismiss him. The duties and responsibilities of his new office remained purposefully hazy and ill-defined. That made it possible for him to concern himself with any matter that aroused his fancy. Beside military and foreign affairs, the central government in Berlin also reserved for itself such vital functions as the postal service, railways and the telegraph. That left the lesser kings very little to say and ample time for pleasure.

Though Bismarck continued to dress in military garb, his main ambition was now to keep the peace. "Germany is saturated," he declared. The goal was reached. From now on all efforts had to be directed toward keeping and consolidating the gains. Order was the number one requirement. Any upset, whether inside or outside the borders, could only endanger the system.

For the next twenty years Bismarck employed his genius in the preservation of peace, and he was successful even beyond the limit of his life-span. No major war erupted between 1871 and 1914. Whatever his motives were, for this accomplishment the world is in his debt.

Did he feel any remorse over the bloodshed of the past? Once, during one of his melancholic spells, he said in the tone of a confessing sinner, "Without me three great wars would not have happened and eighty thousand men had not perished. Parents, brothers, sisters and widows would not be bereaved and plunged into mourning." But these moments of self-criticism passed quickly as he reassured himself that whatever he did was God's will.

As he saw it, peace for Germany required two foundations. First, new treaties of alliance were needed so that, when danger threatened, the country would not have to face more than one enemy at a time. Second, Germany's armor had to be kept so formidable that anybody in his right mind would think twice before attacking her.

The forging of formal and informal diplomatic ties remained Bismarck's chief interest, but he did not forget the armor. Far from abandoning the sword which had wounded France so painfully, he decided to keep it sharpened and ever ready. The compulsory draft was extended to all new parts of the empire. After finishing their active service, the veterans remained members of the reserve system, the *Landsturm,* till they reached the age of forty-five. During regular maneuvers and refresher courses the indoctrination into the Prussian militaristic spirit continued. Men in uniform considered themselves the cream of creation. Reserve lieutenants strutted about like little gods. The sublimity of war was painted in glowing colors while peace, though unavoidable, was held to be an unfortunate period of stagnation.

Before the *Reichstag* the Chancellor thundered, "He who attacks the German nation, will find it armed to a man, and every soldier with the firm conviction in his heart that God is with us." Applauding wildly, the deputies granted him all the funds he requested, not just for one year, but for the next seven, and so voluntarily gave up all control over military matters.

The glorification of war had very unfortunate effects which have been tragically hard to eradicate ever since. Germans began to consider themselves soldiers first and citizens second. Fighting words and fighting gestures became the order even in civilian life. The art of friendly disagreement was lost and the air of internal politics poisoned. Teachers taught a new type of history filled exclusively with war and victory.

The world outside Germany was first puzzled, then frightened. An arms race resulted, dividing Europe into hostile blocks eager to test their military hardware. No longer did small professional armies face each other, as in the past, but now whole nations were in arms. The age of total war was approaching.

Bismarck was inimitable in making the best use of the moment, but he lacked foresight. With his usual acid scorn he rejected any proposals of mutual disarmament as "confused humanitarian ideas."

The state became an extension of the military establishment. Just as the soldier was directed, not only how to shoot, but also how to shine his shoes and fold his blanket, so the civilian was cast into a rigid mold by the authoritarian system. It became the model of the modern totalitarian state.

How did the new nation pay for all this military extravagance? Many a country has been ruined by its voracious soldiery. Not so Germany. Her political unification coincided with a period of fantastic economic growth. The country was catching up with the Industrial Revolution. German scientists wrought miracles in their chemical and optical laboratories. German steamship lines crossed all oceans, and German banks bulged with the profits of rich tycoons and with the savings of frugal craftsmen and white collar workers. The birth rate soared so high that the excess population spilled over into North and South America. In some years over a quarter of a million Germans migrated across the Atlantic Ocean.

The city of Berlin strove hard to merit its new role as the capital of a fifty-odd million empire. Incessantly the noise and dust of new construction assailed the senses. The streets were now paved, and at night the greenish light of gas lanterns kept the military men and the students promenading late. The university had grown into one of the foremost research institutes, particularly in the natural sciences. Theater and opera flourished. Artists and musicians found their way to Berlin from the older cultural centers, such as Vienna, Munich and Weimar.

The mechanism of government ran smoothly and efficiently. The legislative bodies were wax in the Chancellor's hand. He manipulated the deputies so easily that a member of the opposition mournfully described the *Reichstag* as "a figleaf to cover the nakedness of autocracy."

Once when Parliament showed signs of balking at some additional military expenditures, Bismarck had a French customs inspector lured across the border and arrested on a trumped-up charge. The French press reacted with predictable cries of outrage. Triumphantly the Chancellor read to the assembly excerpts from the angry Paris journals. Having created this artificial war scare, he had no more financial problems. As soon as the little storm had blown over, the French official was quietly spirited back into his homeland.

But the great man was not infallible, though many thought him to be. In the first decade of his rule over a united Germany he made two enormous blunders, both in domestic politics, the stepchild among his interests. One had to do with religion and the other with social problems. For neither had he ever shown any deep understanding.

Originally Prussia was an overwhelmingly Protestant state. As it grew, some largely Catholic areas were added. With the founding of the empire, the Catholic population swelled even more, though it remained a minority. The Emperor was a devout Lutheran, and so, in his way, was Bismarck. Three hundred years earlier, they would have insisted that everybody adopt the faith of the ruler. But those days were gone forever. Yet a bitter conflict broke out, not so much on religious beliefs, as on the question of whether man's highest allegiance was to his state or to his church.

Pope Pius IX, an extreme traditionalist, had just condemned all modern scientific and social ideas in blistering terms. On top of this, the Vatican Council proclaimed in 1870 the dogma of papal infallibility. From then on every Catholic was bound to acknowledge that on matters of faith and morals the Pope in Rome spoke with divine authority. His word had to be obeyed as the absolute truth. Any other attitude was sinful.

For Bismarck this doctrine was an intrusion into the power of the state. If the Pope's word was final, he could overrule the government, and the good Catholic had to obey him rather than his Emperor.

The Chancellor's attack was so ferocious that one must look for other reasons beside his dislike of Catholic teachings. It was, after all, very unlikely that the Pope would find many occasions to oppose the German government. What made Bismarck really fighting mad was a fresh challenge to his domination of the *Reichstag*.

A new political party had appeared, the Center, which claimed to represent the German Catholics. But it also had Protestant members, mainly those who felt aggrieved by the imperial government. The Center thus became a new rallying point for the dissatisfied. Every election strengthened its parliamentary delegation.

Real opposition was something the Chancellor could not stomach. It was a personal affront, and he blamed the whole Catholic religion for it. The struggle which arose between the chief executive and a large part of the people is described in the history books under the misleading heading, *Kulturkampf* (cultural struggle).

The government went into battle with all the might at its disposal. Civil marriage was made compulsory. Sermons were censored. Strong fetters were put on Catholic education, since authoritarian rulers always insist that the children belong to the state and have to be trained to give it their undivided loyalty. Therefore church schools and seminaries had to submit to strict government controls or face closure. State examinations were also introduced for prospective priests, and foreign-trained clergymen were ousted from their pastorates.

All this had an entirely unexpected effect. German Catholics, who had been strongly divided on the Pope's ideas, closed ranks and fought back with a tenacity which surprised Bismarck. The force of conviction and faith was something new to the man whose dogma was power and expediency.

Religion thrives on persecution. Bishops, priests and laymen in large numbers went to jail in defiance of the restricting ordinances. Monks and nuns closed their convents rather than submit. Since the state withheld the financial support it customarily granted all religions, generous private donations paid all church expenses. Even so, hundreds of parishes were without pastors. Neither baptisms nor wedding ceremonies could be performed. But the passive resistance continued, and the Center Party, which had been the cause of all the harassment, grew steadily in size.

Bismarck realized finally that he had completely misjudged the strength man derives from his spiritual resources. He saw himself lampooned by the foreign press. His image as the all-powerful master of a nation was slipping. In the ensuing years most of the restrictions were quietly removed, or they were fogotten for lack of enforcement. The *Kulturkampf* was Bismarck's first defeat after a string of stunning victories.

✠ 13 ✠

THE CHANCELLOR SEES RED

EVEN MORE DISASTROUS THAN THE BATTLE WITH THE CATHOLIC Church was the ill-advised crusade against socialism. In the race for industrial superiority Germany was rapidly closing in on England and the United States. The more numerous the smokestacks that belched their evil fumes skyward, the larger became the ranks of the industrial workers, the proletariat. The men behind the machines had hardly any share in the general prosperity. Looking at the display of luxury by the newly rich, they considered any gains they were making too skimpy. The ideas of Karl Marx had now become widespread among the more intelligent workingmen. Though they did not heed the clarion call to violent revolution, they demanded loudly to be allotted more of the wealth they were producing in the grimy factories.

Ferdinand Lassalle was dead, but his revered picture still hung in many a worker's flat. Inspired by his memory, the Social Democratic Party lived on and grew rapidly, led by such articulate spokesmen as August Bebel and Karl Liebknecht. Once Bismarck had toyed with the idea of a combined aristocratic-proletarian front against the liberal middle class, the bourgeoisie. But now the growing strength of the labor movement worried him too much. It stood for complete equality, and this was not at all to the Junker's liking. What common ground could he find with people who were against the military and against the privileges of wealth and birth?

What was even more ominous, the socialists maintained close ties with their brothers in other countries who had joined the "International," led by Marx. This was a workers' organization which transcended boundary lines. Its symbol was the red flag. In the eyes of the Imperial Chancellor this was the ultimate in dangerous unpatriotic defiance. Germans should honor only one flag: the black-white-red colors of the empire.

Bismarck proposed new bills singling out socialist leaders and journalists for special treatment. Their rights to free expression were to be even more curtailed than those of German citizens in general. The majority of the *Reichstag* was by no mean sympathetic to socialism, but to guard their scanty, hard-won privileges, they threw out the bills.

The Chancellor was furious. Impatiently he waited for the right moment to smash the socialists and, at the same time, to punish the recalcitrant Parliament, especially the liberals who were showing signs of independent thought again.

As so often, he was absent from the capital, keeping a tight check on government affairs from his country seat.

A secretary of the chancery arrived at Varzin on a most urgent mission. "I must see the Chancellor immediately," he told Johanna von Bismarck.

"He is out walking in the woods and won't be back for several hours." She was quite annoyed about the intrusion of politics into the serenity of Varzin. "Can't you leave him alone when he is trying to get back his strength out here?"

But the man from Berlin was gone. He rushed out to find his boss. Fighting for breath, he finally spied the lonely figure with the slouch hat and the heavy walking cane, followed closely by his monstrous Great Danes. He resembled the rugged oaks under which he was striding.

"A highly important report, Your Serene Highness," gasped the perspiring official.

"Out here in the forest?" Bismarck felt this to be a desecration of this piece of unspoiled nature. "Can't it wait till I get back to the house?"

"I am afraid not. His Majesty has been gravely wounded."

"Give it to me. Quick."

He tore the paper from the visitor's hand. His cheeks turned crimson. The eyes protruded even more than usual. With mounting agitation he scanned the lines.

The Emperor's carriage had been rolling along on the boulevard Unter den Linden. Suddenly a sniper opened fire from a window. Bleeding profusely from the impact of thirty shotgun pellets, the old man had been rushed back to the palace. The assassin was a mentally deranged university graduate from a well-to-do family. When police stormed the building, he quickly turned the weapon against himself.

The Chancellor looked up from the paper. A smile played on his lips. "Now we've got the scoundrels where we want them."

"The socialists, Your Serene Highness?"

"Oh, those too, but I mean the liberals, the whole parliamentarian pack."

The face of the perplexed bureaucrat was blank. He could not follow the quick logical jumps of that fertile brain which was now bursting with ideas.

"I'll send the *Reichstag* packing immediately."

He did not know how gravely his sovereign was wounded or whether he was even alive. At the moment the fate of the man to whom he owed his position was forgotten. He had perceived a splendid way to exploit the incident for the punishment of his adversaries.

William recovered, but whatever the state of the Emperor's health, Bismarck now had his long-desired weapon. Without the shadow of proof he blamed the socialists for the murder attempt. Beyond that, he even managed to saddle the whole *Reichstag* with the blame. Had they not rejected his antisocialist bills, he told the press, the Emperor would have been better protected.

Parliament was dissolved. In the election campaign the government forces played up the specter of a sinister socialist conspiracy aiming at further assassinations and general lawlessness. Patriotic emotions were stirred up against those red criminals. They had

dared lay hands on the sacred person of the Emperor, who personi-
fied the greatness of the new nation. The German voters responded
like the well-drilled soldiers most of them were at heart. They
trounced the moderates.

In 1879 a more virulent antisocialist bill was presented to the
Reichstag. This time, still under the impact of the shots on Unter
den Linden, the majority adopted it.

An era of persecution began. Socialist publications were confis-
cated, printing shops were raided, presses destroyed. Informers plied
their despicable trade. Thousands landed in prison. Others hurriedly
fled across the borders.

But as in the *Kulturkampf*, Prussian police boots could not stamp
out ideas. The workers, who were by no means bloodthirsty rebels,
met in the woods, in lonely quarries, in the backrooms of inns.
Though unable to campaign openly, the party kept on gaining votes.
Bismarck had another defeat on his record.

But the Chancellor's mind could turn somersaults when the
straight way proved to be unattractive. Convinced now that brute
force was not the answer, he tried an approach reminiscent of the
American saying, "If you can't lick 'em, join 'em." Not that he enrolled as a member of the Social Democratic Party, but with a
stroke of the pen he appropriated some of the most cherished planks
in the opponent's platform.

Years ago, he had ventilated with Lassalle thoughts about insurance against the hazards of industrial work. Now, over his signa-
ture, materialized the first comprehensive social security system in
the world. Compulsory accident, sickness and old age insurance gave
the German worker protection against the many dangers he faced
in making his living. Bismarck's remarkable insurance program became a widely imitated model. Most countries have since adopted
similar programs.

What had prompted the lifelong autocrat to take such a revolutionary step? His wrath against the socialists alone does not explain
it. We must remember that he was not against the workingman as
such. He had always gotten along well with his peasants. For the

poor he harbored a condescending sympathy as long as they did not question his authority. It was an attitude similar to the affection he held for his dogs. Those creatures never forgot who was the master.

The insurance program was, first of all, meant to take the wind out of the socialist sails. The worker should realize that the state was looking out for him. There was no need to rebel. Just be a good, subservient subject of your government, and you will be properly rewarded. An originally revolutionary demand had been turned into a benevolent gift. As Bismarck himself explained, "One who can look forward to an old-age pension, is far more contented and much easier to manage. . . . Money thus spent is well invested; it is used to ward off a revolution which would cost a great deal more."

It was all to the good, only it did not have the effect Bismarck had hoped for. Far from committing suicide on account of the Chancellor's munificence, the Social Democratic Party continued to grow. When the man of blood and iron finally faded from the scene, it was stronger than ever.

Such experiences taught Bismarck that unmitigated despotism was definitely going out of fashion. Parliament, political parties, opposition papers, all these paraphernalia of an incipient democracy, were here to stay. It was far less exerting to work with them than against them. Sometimes hate clouded his sound judgment, but when such moments passed, he found himself thinking that the day might not be distant when he would desperately need the support of the common people and their representatives. With growing apprehension he regarded the Hohenzollern throne. Any day now could find a new emperor occupying it. The Crown Prince mistrusted him, and his wife regarded him with ill-disguised hostility. To stay in power after the crown had passed onto a new head might prove an immensely difficult job. At that moment, political allies, especially from the ranks of Parliament, could make all the difference. It was worth a few friendly gestures, an occasional show of sociability.

In the capital the Bismarcks now occupied a stately palace befitting the Chancellor's rank and world standing. It stood amidst a formal garden which was surrounded by a gold-tipped wrought-iron fence. The offices were much more spacious than the old ones in Wilhelmstrasse. Above them, overlooking a good part of the city, were the parlors and reception rooms with their balconies and French windows. Still farther up could be found the bedrooms and the servants' quarters. Everything was decorated in a flowery overornateness. Prince Otto and his wife preferred old-fashioned decor and frowned on new technical gadgets. In the whole building not a single telephone could be found, not even on the Chancellor's desk, though this invention of Alexander Graham Bell's was already being used in other capitals.

The older the First Minister became, the less he was inclined to go out and receive the hospitality of others. But he loved to have company at home, and nobody dared refuse his invitation.

On the nights indicated in the embossed invitation cards, the palace was ablaze with lights from gas jets, oil lamps set in heavy chandeliers and from innumerable candles in silver candelabra. Through the rooms moved a steady stream of military and civilian dignitaries. Parliamentarians chatted with industrialists, newspapermen with members of the legal profession. Even a sprinkling of professors could be found despite the host's well-known aversion to the academic spokesmen. But he drew a line when it came to poets and artists. He had no use for either their persons or their work. Whatever could be discovered inside the palace or on the grounds in the way of paintings or sculptures was either long out of date or completely hideous.

Bismarck liked it best when he could give a *Herrenabend*, a stag night. At the door he greeted all the men with as much friendliness as his haughty nature would allow. Each guest was addressed by his proper title, such as *Herr Baron, Herr Geheimrat* or *Herr Professor.* Whether in uniform or in civilian knee-length frockcoats, the men perspired freely in the overheated rooms. Only the host and his tropical plants found the temperature pleasant.

On one agreeable feature the Prince's guests could always count. The sideboards were loaded to capacity with gargantuan quantities of food for the buffet supper. Venison from his own estates, meat, fish and poultry, and also big Pomeranian potatoes were the home products. But German nationalism did not prevent the presence of caviar from Russia, oysters from France, English kippers and Spanish sardines.

After heaping their plates with solid food, the gentlemen gladly helped themselves to the liquid refreshments which had also been supplied as if everybody were about to die from thirst. If the Chancellor had not made his mark in history otherwise, he could have claimed the distinction of having made beer respectable at high-class gatherings, whereas before it had been restricted to taverns and student hangouts. In the biggest hall of the palace huge kegs of beer stood against the walls, all gifts from admiring Bavarian brewers, and the visitors filled their own mugs from the spigots.

Finally all guests had filled their stomachs to capacity and slaked their thirst with the foaming brew. Now they crowded into the library, a large, but disorderly room with newspapers all over the floor just as the master of the house had dropped them. He lowered himself into an outsize armchair covered with an ugly cretonne. Contentedly he puffed at his long meerschaum pipe, adopted under protest when the doctor forbade him the strong cigars he had favored in earlier years.

A tight circle formed around him. No effort was needed to keep the conversation going. The Prince took care of it singlehandedly. He kept up an endless soliloquy of anecdotes about the wars, the diplomatic conferences, the meetings with the great and the near-great which animated his life. Who else could draw upon such intimate firsthand knowledge of the foremost secrets of the time? The listeners first gasped in astonishment, then laughed with relief as they heard the rulers and statesmen from their own and other countries lampooned with unbelievable frankness. Restraint in conversation had never been one of Bismarck's virtues, except when he was, so to speak, on the job and found it necessary to conceal his true feelings.

This was how Bismarck liked to carry on a conversation. His talk glowed with witticisms, with funny phrases and imaginative comparisons, while the partners, or rather the audience, accompanied the recital with loud guffaws of hilarity and with vigorous nods of approval. Many of those present would have come regardless of the quality of food and entertainment. They wanted favors, or their positions and fortunes depended on the Chancellor's continued good will. But for whatever reason they were there, they spent an exhilarating evening. The few who liked him, the many who hated him and the remainder who never understood what he was up to—they all agreed that in those palatial but tasteless rooms they were in the presence of greatness.

When they finally left the chancery, many negotiating their way with some difficulty, they were all proud that their country had produced a genius of such magnificence.

✠ 14 ✠

HONEST BROKER

The doctor had finished his examination. Now he had a few questions to ask.

"What did you have for supper last evening, Your Serene Highness?"

"Oh, let me see. Some eggs, eight I believe, with black bread, cheese and pickles. Then three or four herring, you know, the special kind I like. People now call them Bismarck Herring. For dessert we had ices, very good. I lost track of the number I ate."

"No wonder you had stomach cramps during the night and could not sleep. And how much did you drink?"

"My usual mixture of ale and champagne."

"How many glasses?"

"Now listen, young man. I am not used to being questioned like a suspect at the police station. In this country I ask the questions, and people tell me what they know or think they know."

"Very well, if Your Serene Highness resents answering questions, I suggest that you consult a veterinarian. They never ask their patients anything."

With that the physician packed up his satchel and made ready to leave.

The Chancellor let out a roar of laughter. "Not so fast, young man. I rather like your impertinence. Stay. You and I will get along all right." Turning to a servant, he ordered, "Get the doctor's

things out of the carriage and make a guestroom ready for him."
Dr. Ernst Schweninger stayed, and he proved to be a competent
practitioner with a talent for handling difficult patients. With ad-
vancing age, Bismarck's real and imaginary ills were becoming
more bothersome. A number of doctors had fled in exasperation
never to return, driven off by the patient's lack of cooperation and
by the general confusion which often reigned in the household.

It took a disciplinarian of Dr. Schweninger's type to succeed
where others had failed. He almost became a member of the family.
He controlled the daily schedule of eating and sleeping, and his
veto on unwholesome dishes was final. At dinnertime, when the
head of the family called for a particularly strong red wine, the
medic ordered the horrified servant, "You take it right back where
it came from." The master grumbled something unintelligible, but
did not rescind the order.

It is notable that Dr. Schweninger was a Jew, and so was Gerson
Bleichröder, Bismarck's financial adviser, one of the few persons in
whom he had complete confidence. Jews could be found in prominent official positions and in many spheres of public life. The Age
of Bismarck was remarkably free from anti-Semitism, which had a
long tragic history in Germany. The Chancellor declared himself
in favor of religious intermarriage, saying not too delicately that
very good results should come from the mating of "a German Chris-
tian stallion with a Jewish mare." This was a far cry from the anti-
Jewish speeches the budding politician had once made.

With a few exceptions, such as Bleichröder and Schweninger, his
distrust of mankind in general increased as the years passed. Only
the friendship with John Motley withstood the dry rot of time. His
companion of student days was now a highly respected historian.
They exchanged letters throughout their lives. Motley's occasional
visits to Varzin were for both men sources of unmixed joy. The
American scholar's profound admiration of the Mad Junker never
wavered.

Otherwise Bismarck treated the people who flitted in and out
of his life with utter disdain. He was unable to laugh at himself.

Therefore he regarded any criticism as a personal insult. Even cartoonists and humorists encountered the full blast of his ire. It became a crime punishable by prison sentences to speak or write in hostile terms about the Imperial Chancellor. Opposition was equated with treason. Only a few public figures dared challenge the mighty autocrat publicly. One of them was Ludwig Windthorst, leader of the Center Party, who declared, "The Chancellor is not the state. Until now no minister has been so presumptuous as to call his opponents enemies of the state."

To speak such words in the halls of Parliament required considerable courage, for Bismarck was a passionate hater. "I lie awake nights hating," he confessed. He could pursue the objects of his hate long after they had ceased to play any role of public significance. More than one hapless person who crossed him was actually hounded to death. Count Harry von Arnim, the German ambassador to Paris, had very imprudently let it slip that he would not mind being considered Bismarck's successor when the first Chancellor was ready for retirement. That was his undoing. His boss set spies upon him who not only followed his every step but also rifled his desk. Arnim was expelled from the foreign service. Still Bismarck's thirst for vengeance was not sated. The Count was arrested and tried on felony charges for keeping a document which he was to have surrendered to the ministry. Normally such a minor breach of regulations would have been settled through a written reprimand. But Arnim was convicted in open court. To escape prison he fled into exile and died a broken man.

Bismarck's hatred did not even end at the grave. Eduard Lasker, a brilliant lawyer, was the universally esteemed leader of the liberals in the *Reichstag*. Courageously he opposed all attempts to limit personal freedom, and often his strong pleas succeeded in moderating, to some extent, Bismarck's harsh measures. He was a real thorn in the Chancellor's flesh. During a tour of America, Lasker died of a heart attack. Sorrowed by the passing of this prominent visitor, the United States Congress adopted a resolution expressing its regret and asking the German government that this regret be conveyed to the *Reichstag*. Bismarck refused to transmit this resolution to the legislative body. Instead, he sent it back to Washington with the remark, "Am I to make myself my enemy's postman?" No wonder the American press called this callous disregard of common courtliness "malicious, resentful and ill-mannered."

Parliamentarians, such as Lasker, could at least talk back to the Iron Chancellor, though they incurred some risks doing so. But completely under the whip of the Pomeranian slavedriver were all the officers of the executive branch, even those of ministerial rank. The constitution had only provided for one federal executive, the Chancellor. But since he could not possibly attend personally to all the details of imperial government, a cabinet of ministers had gradually developed. But the ministers were Bismarck's creatures, handpicked by him and holding their positions only as long as the sun of his favor shone upon them.

So he sat in dictatorial grandeur behind his specially made oversize desk. Everything around him had to be outsize, even the pencils he used. When he gave orders or listened to reports, the two canine brutes were always lying at his feet like giant black bodyguards ready to tear the intruder apart at a glance from their master.

His iron control extended to members of the family. To be a son of the great man was anything but an unmixed blessing. Bill had inherited his father's appetite, but not his stature nor his ambition. He was fat and lazy. Willing to fill whatever spot the Prince would select for him, he finally settled into the comfortable but unexciting existence of a provincial official.

Herbert, the firstborn, however, was being groomed for bigger things. The father quite obviously hoped to establish a Bismarck dynasty in the imperial chancery. There were precedents in history. The Carolingians, of whom Charlemagne became the most celebrated member, were, for several generations, chief administrators of kings, and the Shoguns of Japan played a similar role.

The wish never reached fulfillment. Herbert worked in the Foreign Office as his father's confidential secretary and was sent out on delicate diplomatic missions. But the old man's hand rested heavily on him. He was never more than a glorified servant expected to obey commands explicitly and receiving a scolding when he did not perform to satisfaction. "Don't talk drivel, Herbert," the Chancellor would shout in the presence of assorted councilors and secretaries.

Finally the imperious patriarch destroyed his son's happiness completely. The younger Bismarck fell in love with the beautiful Princess Elisabeth Carolath, a lady who moved in the most exclusive circles and attracted droves of male admirers. She was unhappily married, and after Herbert proposed to her, she arranged a divorce. When the father heard of it, an explosion of wrath shook the walls of the chancery. Alternately roaring with fury and sobbing in self-pity, the Prince called his son an ingrate. Under no circumstances would he agree to this marriage because the young lady was related to men who opposed him in public life.

Bismarck let fly with all weapons at his command. He threatened to disinherit his son, to fire him from his position and have him blacklisted anywhere in Germany. Finally he announced that he would commit suicide if Herbert persisted. That did it. The son possessed neither the talent nor the stamina of the father. Too weak to face life on his own resources, he renounced his love and eventually married an Austrian countess selected by his father.

The family tyrant probably never realized that he had broken his son's spirit. Torn by remorse, disgusted with himself, Herbert found himself condemned by his associates as a man without backbone. To the contempt which he encountered everywhere he responded with increasingly coarse behavior. The bottle became his chief comforter. Both sons were taken by death when still in their fifties.

Sons, colleagues, even crowned heads, all were mere pieces which the master of Varzin and Friedrichsruh moved around on his chessboard with little regard for their feelings. His game was and remained power politics. All else had to be subordinated.

Germany's relations with the outside world were Bismarck's own personal concern, and woe to those who dared interfere. Violently he resented any meddling in foreign affairs on the part of Parliament. "Foreign policy," he said, "is difficult enough anyhow. It can only become more confused by three hundred asses," meaning the three hundred members of the *Reichstag*.

Continued peace for his country was now his foremost goal. The nation had reached what he considered her God-given boundaries. All that was left was to guard them day and night. As long as he was at the helm, Germany would never willingly go to war again.

But this determination was not enough. He had to look beyond the frontier gates and see that no armed conflict broke out anywhere in the neighborhood. Once a major fire erupted in one building, it might get out of control and envelop others in the neighborhood. Therefore fire prevention was the best course.

The term "preventive war" could not be found in Bismarck's dictionary, though some military men were all for hitting a potential enemy before he could muster enough strength. He considered such a step clumsy and dangerous. This was to admit the failure of the diplomatic process, something he would never concede.

To preserve the peace was a task which required infinitely more refined skill than to wage war. It required genius.

To look at the world situation during the Age of Bismarck is to see how aspirations overlapped, how claims and counterclaims intertwined and formed a pattern so complex that only the best minds could understand, let alone modify, it. Consider the largest countries, since they were the only ones that mattered:

The United States of America:
Protected by two oceans, she still tended, for the most part, to her own business and stayed away from foreign entanglements. Bismarck did not have to bother about Uncle Sam.

Great Britain:
Her strength lay in her colonial empire. Her navy had no rival on the seas. She coveted no further possessions on the European continent and favored there a balance of power maintained by several countries of about equal strength. But she was very determined to keep European rivals away from what she considered

her "spheres of influence"—namely, France from Africa and Russia from southern Asia and from the Mediterranean. With the new Germany she had no quarrel.

France:

The deep wounds of 1871 had stopped bleeding, and the nation had made a startling economic recovery. France was once more in the first league of world powers. Patriots were passionately clamoring for revenge. To divert their attention from Alsace-Lorraine, Bismarck actively encouraged French statesmen to find solace in African and Far Eastern colonies. Otherwise he did his best to keep France in diplomatic quarantine.

Italy:

Like Germany a newly united nation, she was still weak, both economically and militarily, unable to initiate a strong foreign policy of her own. But her nationalists loudly agitated for the "liberation" of Austrian territory in the Southern Alps where the Italian language was spoken.

Austria:

Still a great power, though definitely past her peak. Barred from any significant role in the German world, she was now angling for new land and new glory in the southeast corner of Europe. There, on the Balkan Peninsula, lived and intermingled many different nationalities which were continually engaged in bitter feuding with each other.

Russia:

A clumsy giant, just beginning to feel his strength and looking for worlds to conquer, especially south of the Black and Caspian Seas and, also, in the Balkan Peninsula. Russia's fondest dream was, as it had been for centuries, to capture the straits leading from the Black to the Mediterranean Seas. They were at the moment in Turkish hands.

Turkey:

A crumbling empire, aptly called the Sick Man of Europe. Unable to defend herself against the wolfpack which threatened her borders, she had become a danger to peace because of her very helplessness. The Balkan Peninsula was being torn from her grasp, piece by piece, by powers arguing fiercely among themselves over the loot.

This was the stormy ocean of conflicting aims and desires in which Bismarck attempted to navigate. Only he could do it. Inflammable fuel floated on several spots, and it had to be kept from igniting.

England and France competed for colonies, but were united in mistrusting Russia's designs on Constantinople.

Austria's and Russia's plans for mastery of the Balkan Peninsula clashed head-on.

Turkey cried for help against Russian attack.

Those were only the major sources of trouble. Many minor ones complicated the picture further.

Bismarck was quite happy to see the other powers quarrel among themselves. That kept their eyes averted from German lands. In fact, by his underhanded tricks, he fanned the little flames of irritation, but he stood guard to see that they did not get out of hand. It was a dangerous game. In some sports contesting players find themselves suddenly united in attacking the umpire. This can happen also in international politics. One of the Chancellor's cardinal principles was never to alienate more than one power at a time if alienation could not be prevented.

In his own words, Bismarck became the "honest broker" of Europe, though his friend Bleichröder caustically remarked that the two terms were really contradictory. As an oversize dove of peace, the Iron Chancellor attempted with all the finesse and energy at his disposal to keep the great powers from each other's throats.

The most difficult phase of the peace-keeping operation was to prevent an out-and-out clash between Germany's two big neighbors, Austria and Russia. In 1878 such a collision was imminent. Vienna and St. Petersburg were preparing for a showdown while both

England and France were standing by to see what might be in it for them. A thunderstorm was gathering over Europe which threatened to assume the proportions of a world war.

Now Bismarck rose majestically to play the self-assigned role of all-European referee. He called on all involved parties to come to him and talk out their differences. The Congress of Berlin was one of history's outstanding summit meetings. No such galaxy of notables had assembled in one place since the Congress of Vienna sixty-three years earlier.

From the gables of the chancery fluttered the flags of all the invited nations. An honor guard was drawn up on both sides of the big gate leading through the park to the broad steps of the main building. Onlookers crowded on the opposite sidewalk held in line by policemen with long sabers which were always getting entangled between their legs. With difficulty they kept the driveway free for the gilded carriages with their liveried board-stiff coachmen as they drove slowly through the gate.

"Here comes the Austrian Prime Minister," an experienced celebrity-watcher announced. "The footmen wear black and yellow, the Austrian colors."

"Who is the blond fellow with the red fez on his head?" somebody wanted to know. "You can hardly see the color of his coat under all the gold embroidery."

"This is the Turkish Foreign Minister," lectured the expert. "He is really a German, but the job in Constantinople pays well, as you can see for yourself."

The domed central hall with its pillars and marble busts was the scene of the formal meetings. Bismarck, resplendent in a white gala uniform, presided over this gathering of government chiefs, foreign ministers and their large staffs. Everybody recognized his authority as the host and supreme moderator. For a whole month the sessions continued. But more real progress was made outside the big hall, when the diplomats stuck their heads together by twos and threes, probing and bargaining. This informal type of politicking was mostly carried on in drawing room corners during the countless receptions and glittering balls which seemed to be the unavoidable by-products of such occasions.

Three old men dominated the scene. The least effective of the three was Prince Gortschakoff, the Russian Premier, now an eighty-year-old ruin who had to be carried to the sessions. For many decades he had sparred with Bismarck, and there was no love lost between the two experienced practitioners of intrigue and deceit. Now the fires were nearly burned out. Plagued by the gout, the Russian had trouble keeping awake during the endless haggling. Still he represented a power to be reckoned with.

In contrast, Disraeli, the leader of Queen Victoria's government, was still the elegant man of the world. His hair and beard were carefully groomed and tinted black. His frockcoat with broad silken cravat and diamond-studded pin was immaculate. As a concession to his age, however, he walked with the help of a slender gold-tipped cane.

The sixty-three-year-old Bismarck looked as old as the Englishman, who was almost ten years his senior. Each was a genius in his own right; each had created an empire. But the interests of their countries lay far apart; the avenues of their political designs did not intersect. So they could, without any misgivings, enjoy the spirited conversational give-and-take in which they were both grand masters. The two learned quickly to appreciate each other. They met for intimate dinners and talked into the late hours of the night. Disraeli even honored his host by accepting from him a cigar, though he detested smoking.

The Congress of Berlin averted an armed encounter, at least for the time being, and Bismarck was the man of the day, the savior of Europe. Actually the crack had not been filled in, but only thinly papered over. Thirty-six years later, the First World War was to begin at the same spot and practically over the same issues that had plagued the diplomats in Berlin.

As usual, the negotiators completely forgot to consider the wishes and sensibilities of the Serbs, Bulgarians, Croats, Bosnians and the many other nationalities living in the Balkans. They simply drew lines across a map of which many of them had only a very faint knowledge. "Here, you can push your weight around on this side of the line," they told Russia, though not in such direct language. Austria received, more or less, a free pass to do likewise on the other side.

It was a solution which satisfied none of the two antagonists for long. They continued to make threatening noises, and soon both blamed Bismarck for having deprived them of their full desserts. Such is the fate of the honest broker, even if he demands and receives nothing for himself. But there was at least one highly satisfied Congress participant, namely Disraeli. While the Russian bear was busy mauling the Balkan carcass, it would not have time to swallow up the Bosporus and the Dardanelles. The British Premier also received a little bonus by taking over another little colony, the island of Cyprus.

Austrians and Russians growled at each other across their common frontier. Their mood grew uglier with each passing month. Now the Chancellor was certain that, once the two armies clashed in battle, Germany would invariably be drawn into the carnage. His diplomatic schemes grew more complex. A journalist compared his crisscrossing web of alliances, agreements and understandings with the confusing pattern of tracks in a major railway switchyard.

He played a diplomatic trumpcard by concluding a firm alliance with Austria. The wise moderation after the war of 1866 now paid off. By including Italy this pact was enlarged to the famous Triple Alliance in 1882. It formed a block extending from the Baltic to the Mediterranean, clear along the central spine of Europe.

But Austria's main antagonist was Russia, and the Czarist armies with their bottomless pool of manpower were camped all along the wide-open eastern frontier of the *Reich*. To protect the vulnerable flank Bismarck negotiated a highly secret arrangement with Russia, labeled the Reinsurance Treaty. The two treaties clearly cancelled each other out, but this caused their originator no headache. Pacts, though solemnly pledged, were tools to be used and then discarded as the moment demanded it. "No great power can in the long run be guided by a treaty which conflicts with the real interest of the country." With these words Bismarck described the value he himself placed on such pieces of paper.

One loophole which he cleverly left himself was the stipulation that Germany was only obliged to help if her treaty-partner was the victim of aggression. We have since learned how easy it is to define aggression the way it suits the definer.

Against his better judgment, Bismarck was, for a short time, lured into an adventure which ran counter to his master plan. Nationalistic firebrands had long shouted that Germany had to have overseas colonies, since all the big powers had them. They looked at a dependent territory somewhere in Asia or Africa as at a kind of status symbol. The Chancellor had steadfastly refused to go along. When a young hothead brought him a map of Africa and pointed at some inviting blank spots, he answered, "Your map of Africa is very beautiful, but my map of Africa lies in Europe. Here is Russia, and here is France, and we are in the middle. This is my map of Africa."

To acquire some piece of tropical jungle was not worth incurring the enmity of England, which wanted no competition in the dark corners of the world. And Germany had no navy capable of protecting outlying colonies.

Yet the nationalists kept up their agitation, and they received support from industrialists, importers and shipbuilders who saw new possibilities for profit. Finally Bismarck succumbed to the siren call. By 1885 Germany had acquired colonies in East and West Africa and in the South Pacific island world. Then the Chancellor lost all interest in further colonial projects. But the damage was done. His earlier reservations turned out to have been very well taken. England's friendship turned sour, and in 1914, when the test of fire came, the German navy was unable to hold the gains.

The snatching up of stray colonies had been a mistake. Perhaps it was a symptom that the Iron Chancellor's mental powers had passed their peak. Bismarck was convinced that only he could keep the ship on course, that it would surely founder if he retired. Not only did he neglect to groom a successor, but he was suspicious of first-rate minds and surrounded himself with mediocrities who knew better than to propose any ideas of their own. Only flatterers and yes-men could hope for advancement.

People began to ask themselves if the old man was not losing touch with the times. Some of his ideas seemed hopelessly outdated. He read almost nothing, except newspapers and official reports. In the meantime, the German mind was moving in a dangerous direction. This was something over which he had no control, and in the end it proved to be more destructive than any struggle in the Balkans could have been.

Entranced by the meteoric rise of the new empire, philosophers and poets invented a German destiny which amounted to the right of world conquest. Scholarship turned into a handmaiden of overbearing nationalism. Richard Wagner, the composer, and Friedrich Nietzsche, the mad thinker, conceived vague ideas of a Teutonic super-race endowed with special privileges. They overturned Judaeo-Christian morality and proclaimed instead the right of the strong to dominate the weak. Out of this marriage of mysticism with exaggerated self-adoration a monster was conceived which was to darken the twentieth century with unspeakable horror: the monster of Hitlerism.

Bismarck did not foresee this development. His mind was troubled by more immediate concerns. With every passing month it became more difficult to keep the slender structure of peace from collapsing. At the same time, the worries on the homefront increased. The Emperor was nearing his ninetieth birthday. He still carried himself erect. His beard, now snow white, was neatly trimmed and rounded on both cheeks, and the smartly tailored uniforms fitted his slender frame. But his face was now a yellowish waxlike mask. His letters and official notations indicated growing senility. He was completely at a loss to understand his Chancellor's complicated and often contradictory designs.

William I was content to let Prince Bismarck rule in his name. But occasionally he still balked at signing a document or receiving a guest or taking a trip, claiming such an act conflicted with his sense of honor or morality. Then followed almost automatically the often rehearsed sequence of scenes: the threat of resignation, His Majesty's trip to the chancery where he, sobbing childishly, promised to be good and give up his obstinacy, and finally the withdrawal of the resignation. In one of his more lucid moments, William joked, "At best it is not easy to be an emperor under such a chancellor."

But how long could this go on? And what would come afterward? So far the wily Junker had always been able to make the right move at the right moment. He always managed to keep several roads open so that he could proceed in the most advantageous direction; and in the ability to make on-the-spot decisions he had no peer.

But his whole position had been based on his expert handling of the royal sovereign. This relationship would end with the final breath of William I. A completely new situation would arise. Would he be able to master it as he had mastered all previous situations? He did not know, and it worried him. To witness a development without being able to control it was a new experience. His health and his humor suffered, and life became even more miserable for the people who surrounded him.

✠ 15 ✠

DROPPING THE PILOT

THE CHAMBER OF THE *Reichstag* WAS DENSELY PACKED, WHICH only happened when something important was about to break. They were all in their seats, the Conservatives to the right, the Liberals and the Center deputies in the middle, and the Social Democrats to the left. Even the bench reserved for the busy imperial ministers was completely filled with portly gentlemen in starched collars bent over stacks of forbidding-looking papers.

In low tones rumors were passing from row to row, till the presiding officer, high up on his rostrum, rang the little bell which brought the session to order.

"The Imperial Chancellor, His Serene Highness, Prince von Bismarck, desires to make a pronouncement."

A hush settled over the chamber. Nobody had any doubt what the message would be. The moment required the utmost in solemnity and decorum.

Bismarck caught his monocle by the black silken cord and adjusted it to the left eye. His face was pallid. He looked very tired. Slowly he unfolded the paper before him.

"Herr President, Honorable Deputies. I have the sad duty to inform you of a most tragic event."

What they had so long expected had finally occurred. An eerie rustle swept through the hall. As one man the *Reichstag* rose to its feet.

"It has pleased God, the Almighty, to take from us this morning our beloved sovereign, William the First, Emperor of Germany and King of Prussia. May his soul rest in peace."

While the Chancellor was still speaking, the mellow sounds of bells began to filter into the room. One by one, the churches of Berlin took up the plaintive rhythm of the dirge.

The news was received in silence in the chamber. There was no show of emotion. If anything, a sense of relief permeated the assembly, relief that the inevitable had finally occurred. The tension of the last months was now dissolved. Only Bismarck's left hand went up to cover the tears in his eyes. Whatever happened now, on this March day in 1888, the most magnificent period of his life had come to an end. The future was shrouded in uncertainty. A unique bond which had tied two entirely different personalities together in a fateful relationship was broken forever.

The central square was black with people. Black were the flags hanging limply from windows and balconies. The massive portals of the cathedral were draped in black. To the majestic strains of Beethoven's funeral march, six colonels in dress uniform carried the casket out of the sanctuary. Behind it walked an assortment of might and rank as it is seldom assembled in one spot.

The ladies of the house of Hohenzollern were completely veiled in black. The male members wore black bands on the left sleeves of their uniform tunics. Then came visiting kings and reigning dukes, princes and princesses of royal houses, most of them connected by some family relation with the deceased. Ambassadors and military attachés followed, many in exotic garb, and then came the cream of the *Reich's* military and civilian leadership.

As the casket was gently placed on the open hearse, cannon boomed from the parade grounds in a final salute. To the gloomy roll of muffled drums the eight coal-black horses pulled away, directed by outriders in silver-black liveries. The band of the Imperial Guard struck up the mournful, *"Ich hatt' einen Kameraden"* (I had a buddy), the tune which accompanies every German soldier to his grave.

Bareheaded the Berliners watched. They were impressed by the grandiose pageantry, but immediately they discovered that the most important celebrity was missing from the cortege.

"Where is the new Emperor?" many asked.

"That's right. He is not there. He should have walked right behind the casket. I only see the widow and the grandson."

Some spectators knew the reason. It had been whispered about all over the capital. "He is sick. He is a dying man."

"They better not throw away the black flags. Most likely we'll have another funeral before long. And what then?"

The air was full of anxiety. Fear of an uncertain future depressed the general mood even more than the sound of the muffled drums.

Overnight, Crown Prince Frederick William had become Emperor Frederick III. He was fifty-seven years old. Many Germans had been looking forward to being governed by this handsome Prince with the friendly blue eyes and the rich brown beard. His deep humanitarian feeling for the poor and the suffering was well known. He was the darling of Germany's cultural set, which had no stomach for Bismarck's stifling regime nor for the hurrahs of the militarists. With the ascension of the new Emperor, they fervently hoped, a breath of fresh, clean air would sweep across the nation.

When the news of his elevation reached him, Frederick III was not even within the borders of the empire he was to rule. He was a mere shadow of a man, tortured by insufferable pains. The foremost medical authorities of many countries had examined him. Their diagnosis was cancer of the throat. There was no effective cure. All the doctors could do was try to alleviate the intense discomfort. At the moment of his father's death, the patient was resting under the warm sun of the Italian Riviera. Now Bismarck's telegram summoned him back to the raw March winds of Berlin.

Too weak to take his place in the funeral procession, the new Emperor watched from a window of the Charlottenburg Palace as the long line of bespangled carriages, flanked by squadrons of cavalry, passed by on their way to the Hohenzollern mausoleum. Nobody noticed the shrunken face behind the curtains. The neck was swathed in shawls and bandages which hid a silver tube inserted by the doctors to keep their patient from suffocating.

On the next day Bismarck made his first official report to the new sovereign. Unable to speak, the Emperor had to write out his comments in a shaky, almost illegible hand.

Toward evening the Chancellor called the ministers together. They met under a heavy pall of gloom.

"We must prevail on His Majesty to abdicate in favor of his son," advised a cabinet member.

"Yes," counseled another. "What impression will it make on the German people to be ruled by a man who can't even talk?"

But Bismarck was in no hurry. An emperor on the threshold of death meant a chancellor in almost unrestricted command of the empire.

The sick monarch had no energy to oppose any measures his chief executive thought up. Even in small matters Bismarck insisted on having his way. When Frederick wanted to hand out decorations to some of his old associates, the Chancellor prevented it because the views of those people were too liberal to suit him.

But this rather comfortable arrangement could not last much longer. The time had come to consider the present heir to the throne. It was, at most, a matter of months till the crown would pass to William, Frederick's twenty-eight-year-old son. Could the new Crown Prince also be molded into a willing tool of the aging Premier?

The situation looked promising. William had been the favorite of his grandfather, and the first German Emperor had been his model and ideal. With reverence he had adopted the old William's concept of Hohenzollern greatness.

His left arm had been crippled at birth due to some blundering physician or midwife, yet young William was obsessed with fantasies of combat and manly strength as if to overcompensate for his physical defect. Parades, maneuvers, martial ceremonial of all kinds occupied much of his time. The outside world knew him as the man in the narrow-waisted hussar's uniform, sitting stiffly on his horse, the healthy arm raised in the pose of a general calling his men to attack. When he spoke, his vocabulary abounded in expressions of fight and defiance. His favorite companions were the officers of the guard with whom he liked to exchange the gossip and the crude humor of the barracks. Such a person, showing all the distinct signs of emotional inmaturity, was about to be cast in one of the leading roles on the world scene.

An unhappy home life aggravated the unfortunate effects of a physical handicap. William was at odds with his parents, particularly with his English-born mother, whom he subconsciously blamed for his weakness. To spite the daughter of Queen Victoria, he delighted in boisterous nationalistic utterances. His military friends were waiting impatiently for this paladin of German preeminence to ascend the throne and put the "Englishwoman" in her place.

The estrangement between parents and son served Bismarck's purposes well. He did everything he could to deepen the wound. Against the wishes of the father, but backed by the grandfather, whose word was final, William had served a kind of apprenticeship in the Foreign Office. The idea had, of course, been the Chancellor's; he wanted to indoctrinate the young man in the techniques of Bismarckian statecraft. It might have worked out, had William been a better student. But though he possessed considerable ability, his desire to learn was minimal, a fact to which his earlier tutors had given loud testimony.

The reign of the second German Emperor lasted less than a hundred days. Around his deathbed stood the family and the chief servants of the crown. Unable to utter a word, the dying man placed the hand of his wife into that of his Chancellor. It was a pathetic gesture, a plea that the two who had been lifelong enemies should stand together for the sake of the empire.

The soundless plea remained unheeded. Even had Bismarck been willing to forget the past, there was the hostile son, now Emperor William II. Before Frederick had even ceased to breathe, he had given orders to search his mother's private suite for important papers. He suspected her of planning to spirit them out of the country to England. Soldiers stood guard at all entrances. The empress-mother was a prisoner in her own palace.

William II had grown up with a generation which worshipped the name of Bismarck as that of a demigod, a Hercules of superhuman capacities. The new Emperor's expressions of gratitude and continued favor were flowery and exaggerated. For the moment the tenure of the seventy-three-year-old Chancellor seemed assured.

The chancery remained the nerve center of the empire, while the new Emperor was preoccupied with troop inspections and similar pastimes. To listen to the reports of his ministers was a bore for him. As soon as he could he escaped to the officers' club to dine and joke with his old companions.

His special train, painted white and gold, carried him to all important German cities. Then he set out on a pompous round of state visits to various capitals, accompanied by his wife, the Empress Augusta Victoria, and by a large retinue of officers from all branches of the military establishment. Like a conqueror he rode through the streets of Vienna, St. Petersburg and Constantinople saluting the curious masses which were kept at a safe distance by cordons of soldiers. Beaming with pleasure he fingered his black mustache, which had been carefully twirled into two pointed half circles.

Bismark encouraged his sovereign's costly excursions while he himself continued to captain the ship of state. So sure was he of his unimpaired position that he stayed away from Berlin for months at a time. From Varzin and from Friedrichsruh couriers brought his decisions to the capital. Wherever the Chancellor dwelled at the moment was the real seat of government.

This show of self-confidence turned out to be a bad mistake. Bismarck misjudged the personality of his ruler and also the changing character of the times. It was a change he had brought about himself.

He had created a nation in arms. Now it flexed its muscles and put to rest its mind. Louder and louder sounded the Emperor's warlike pronouncements. One of his favorite expressions was the "mailed fist" of Germany which would smash all obstacles. Students and young recruits became infected with this bombastic substitute for serious thought.

The new generation had grown up intoxicated with national splendor and military glory, contemptuous of compassion and intellectual modesty. It became fashionable to ridicule foreign nations. A new vicious brand of anti-Semitism came to the surface. Its chief spokesman was the imperial court chaplain.

The personalities of William II and Otto von Bismarck were moving on a collision course. Both were determined to have their will at all cost. Both had violent tempers and very short nerve ends. Both were convinced that God was in their corner. William II not only called himself "Emperor by the grace of God," he practically considered himself part of the deity. An obsession with a strength he did not possess speaks from the words:

"Remember that the German people are chosen by God. On me as the German Emperor, the spirit of God has descended. I am His weapon, His sword, His vice-regent."

The portents of approaching trouble were ominous, but Bismarck took no precautions, so sure was he that no German ruler could get along without him. Off he went, once more, to his rustic retreat. This time he stayed nearly eight months.

One wintry day a telegram summoned him back to Berlin for a crown council, a meeting of the cabinet presided over by the Emperor himself. Bismarck fumed with anger. Why was William not out reviewing his troops? Why was he butting into the Chancellor's business? Used to always taking the initiative, Bismarck did not like this at all.

The journey was uncomfortable. Shivering with the cold and in a thoroughly black mood, he arrived at the palace, determined to teach the young man a lesson.

At six o'clock in the evening, the waiting ministers were ushered into the conference room which was hung with tapestries depicting battle scenes. They bowed from the hip toward the Emperor and then seated themselves at the long oval table. Despite the blazing lights in the crystal chandeliers, all the faces appeared drawn and old.

William laid before the cabinet a serious domestic problem. The coal miners in Westphalia had gone on strike. There had been clashes with troops. Large-scale disorder threatened. The Emperor's sympathies were all on the side of the underpaid and overworked miners. He was determined to pressure the mine owners into granting living wages and decent working conditions.

"As a first step I am going to abolish Sunday work. Furthermore, no women or children should be hired to go into the pits."

From these practical steps he proceeded to develop a more grandiose idea. "I have decided to convene an international conference on labor problems here in Berlin. The whole situation must be studied in depth. Far-reaching solutions need to be found."

It was a very sensible and far from radical plan. Yet Bismarck rose in wrath to give battle. "Your Majesty's proposal is a surrender to the rabble," he shouted.

In his pent-up anger he gave his sovereign a dressing-down as a schoolmaster scolds a naughty pupil. The man who had made history by creating a social insurance system for the workers, now vehemently opposed the Emperor's concern for the same workers. It was one thing to grant gifts of benevolence to the suffering. It was quite another to give in to threats against the authority of the state. Strikers should be answered with bullets, not promises. Once and for all, the quarrelsome socialists who were behind all this must be taught a lesson. By pampering them, one only encourages them to become more obstinate.

Brushing aside the humane proposals of the ruler, Bismarck demanded martial law and the suspension of the constitution which he himself had written.

William II was horrified. This was not what he had meant when he spoke of Germany's mailed fist. "Do you want to drive the nation into civil war? I won't have it. I will not soil the beginning of my reign with the blood of my own subjects. I am the king of the poor, as well as the rich."

Hurt like a child who had been deprived of a favorite toy, he looked around. "What do the rest of my ministers say to all this? Do you find merit in my proposals?"

The ministers were silent. Nobody dared approve what their chief had rejected. Too long had his hand held them in an iron grip.

"I have no ministers," snarled the humiliated Emperor. "They are all Bismarck's ministers." He was learning fast.

The Chancellor played his old trumpcard. "If Your Majesty insists on such a dangerous course, I don't feel I will be able to continue serving as your chief adviser."

Here was the old weapon again, the threat of resignation. Once more it worked. "We shall have to discuss the matter further," spluttered William and then stormed out of the room. The thin ends of his mustache quivered excitedly against his crimson cheeks.

It was not a complete victory, only a temporary setback for the opponent. There was nothing like the tearful surrender which had been the usual response of the grandfather. The air remained tense, filled with the forebodings of an early showdown. It could only be a matter of days till one of the two stubborn personalities had to yield to the other.

The Chancellor had driven himself into a dead-end street. The will of the ruler had to prevail in the end. Bismarck himself had arranged it so that the Prime Minister's fate depended only on the sovereign's pleasure.

It was bad enough that William dabbled in social problems. But far worse was to come. He began to interfere with the conduct of foreign affairs, and that was the cardinal sin in Bismarck's eyes. While the master chess player could keep several games going at the same time and keep the opponents guessing about his next moves, William was blunt and without finesse. He talked too much and gave too little thought to the consequences.

Ever since he took office, the Chancellor had striven to keep on friendly terms with both Austria and Russia. Now, the new resident of the royal palace continued to assure the Habsburg cousins of his eternal fealty, but he began to throw barbs in the direction of the Czar. His military aides filled him with fears of a Russian attack and hinted at the wisdom of a preventive war.

When the German monarch also began to treat England in a contemptuous manner, the whole intricate net of Bismarckian diplomacy was in danger of being torn to shreds. The Chancellor found that drastic steps were in order to stop the inexperienced amateur on the throne. He dug out a forty-year-old rule which had been gathering dust in the files. According to it, ministers were only allowed to confer with the monarch by permission and in the presence of the Prime Minister. His person was to be the only link between the crown and its lesser servants.

William exploded when he found himself cut off from most sources of information. If he allowed this to go unchallenged, he might as well give up any dream of being more than a crowned figurehead.

He did not have to wait long for an occasion to launch the attack. As the relationship between ruler and Prime Minister neared the crisis stage, Bismarck felt the need to get on better terms with the *Reichstag*. He invited an old political adversary, Windthorst, the leader of the Center Party, for a confidential talk. Perhaps a united front reaching from center to far right could be arranged. When the Emperor found out about this meeting, he was enraged that such an important move should be initiated without his knowledge.

It was the Chancellor's habit to sleep late into the morning. At the ungodly hour of eight, a knock at the bedroom door awakened him. "His Majesty has been waiting for you at the Foreign Office for some time," announced a frightened secretary.

Without taking time to shave, without his customary ample breakfast, an extremely grouchy Bismarck rushed from his official residence to Wilhelmstrasse, which still housed the foreign affairs staff. He found William nervously pacing the floor. Two highly irritated men glared at each other.

Not taking time for formalities, the Emperor snapped, "I hear that Windthorst came to see you. I hope you threw the rascal out."

Bismarck's face was a mask of steel. "No, I consider it my duty to receive members of Parliament who come on important matters of state."

"Even if your sovereign forbids you?" The challenge was direct and knife-sharp.

"Your Majesty's power to command ends at my wife's drawing room."

The proud answer caused the visitor to shift positions. "I must ask you to rescind the order requiring the ministers to see me only in your presence. It is demeaning to my position as the ruling monarch."

"Impossible, Your Majesty. If I am to conduct the affairs of state effectively, I must be in on all deliberations and on all decisions. The rule must prevail as long as I am your chief adviser."

"But how can I wait for your advice when you are away from the capital for months at a time?"

Bismarck's habits, born of haughty self-assurance, were now coming to haunt him. But he remained adamant.

The atmosphere was electric, as before the break of the thunderstorm. Once more William changed the topic and began to talk about Russia. He had heard rumors that Russian troops were massing along the German frontier. Shouldn't something be done about it?

"But first, before ordering any countermeasures, I want to speak directly with the Czar. He has invited me to a hunt. So we will soon see from where the wind blows."

No subject could have been more apt to bring the Chancellor's blood to the boiling point. A personal meeting of the two autocrats was the last thing he wanted. His impetuous master would certainly manage to offend the Czar, and then the whole edifice of German-Russian friendship would come crashing down.

Bismarck toyed with a dispatch case which he had dropped on

the desk before him. It followed him wherever he went. Nobody was allowed to see its contents.

"I advise strongly against such a journey. The Czar's personal feelings about Your Majesty are decidedly unfriendly."

"How so? This is new to me. When he visited me, not so long ago, we had a most cordial get-together."

"Well, I have a secret report here. It recounts how he talked about Your Majesty recently. I cannot let you read it. It would hurt your feelings too much."

The Emperor's curiosity was aroused, as had been expected. He demanded to see the report. After a show of reluctance which was not very convincing, Bismarck handed him the paper.

Hurriedly William's eyes darted over the lines. His face blanched in wordless fury. He found himself described by his cousin in St. Petersburg as an "ill-bred youngster of bad faith."

Shaking with ire, the Emperor rushed out of the room. The fateful interview was over.

On the following day, an embarrassed court adjutant appeared at the chancery. How does one deliver such a message to the man who was a living legend to millions of his contemporaries? He hesitated. He stammered. Finally he blurted out, "His Majesty requests that Your Serene Highness rescind the order concerning the cabinet ministers. Otherwise His Majesty expects you instantly to tender your resignation."

There was only one answer. Twenty-eight years of unprecedented power and success had come to an end. Bismarck sat down to write his letter of resignation. In precise, dignified language, he restated his position on the relationship between monarch and chief minister. Then came the proud conclusion:

From my impressions during the last few weeks, I may humbly assume that by tendering my resignation I am meeting the wishes of Your Majesty and that I may safely count on its being graciously accepted. I should have tendered the resignation of my offices to

Your Majesty long ago had I not been under the impression that
Your Majesty desired to utilize the experience and abilities of a
faithful servant of your predecessors. . . .

William II forbade the publication of this document which was
a little literary masterpiece. The nation was told that Bismarck had
asked to be relieved from the burden of his various offices for reasons of ill health. Hardly anybody in the political world believed it.

The ex-Chancellor drove out to the royal mausoleum in Charlottenburg and placed three roses on the tomb of his old master with
whom he had built an empire.

In March of the year 1890 the Age of Bismarck came to an end.
The British magazine *Punch* published one of the most celebrated
cartoons in the history of journalism. It shows a smug William II
with the crown on his head leaning over the railing of a big ship.
The pilot's ladder has been lowered to the little dinghy riding on
the waves. A grim-faced Bismarck in pea jacket and nautical cap
is descending the ladder. The caption reads:

DROPPING THE PILOT

✠ 16 ✠

FIRST-CLASS FUNERAL

THE BISMARCKS WERE PACKING IN HASTE. HERBERT HELPED HIS
father tie important papers into bundles. Johanna von Bismarck
supervised the wrapping of china and silver. Countless medals,
golden cups, portraits and other gifts from all over the world were
stuffed into boxes. More than one delicate piece broke as servants
were driven to greater speed.

A special problem was posed by the three hundred boxes of cigars
and the thirteen thousand bottles of champagne. The owner insisted
that they follow him into retirement, especially the bottles. He
was still working on the fulfillment of a vow, made many years
ago, to consume fifty thousand bottles of France's most famous product during his lifetime.

Across a corridor the door to an office stood open. Bismarck
could see a man in military uniform working at a desk. It was his
successor, General Leo von Caprivi. The speed with which he had
been installed in the chancery was a sign that the Emperor had no
intention of retreating. On the contrary, by all indications he seemed
very anxious to get the old Junker out of the limelight as fast as
possible.

Contemplating his fate, Bismarck had to admit that he was not
doing so badly despite his fall from power. He was still a prince and
one of the wealthiest landlords in the country. His name was a
household word. Already the books about his life and work

amounted to a sizable library. Not many personalities of his magnitude had survived their exit from the historical scene. One who did was Napoleon, with whom he was often compared. He would have envied the Prussian the splendor and luxury of his retirement years.

Yet Bismarck was not looking forward to a pensioner's life. It was a bitter sight to see things go on without him. No general outcry was heard in protest against his removal. Many Germans had long regarded his regime as an anachronism. It belonged in a time which was fading fast, never to return.

He could not forget for a moment that the retirement was against his will. Though seventy-five years old and plagued by painful ailments, he had wanted to go on indefinitely, an ageless warrior like the giants of Germanic mythology.

Thousands lined the streets through which he rode on his way to the depot. Berliners love to watch a spectacle whether caused by victory, death or the dumping of an old man on the ash heap. On the platform the crowds pressed against the space cleared for the dignitaries who had come to see the former Chancellor off. The diplomatic corps was there in full force. There were parliamentarians and journalists. But the Emperor stayed away, and so did the new chief minister. Many high bureaucrats found it prudent to keep their distance from the man who had fallen from grace.

A detachment of cuirassiers presented arms as he stepped into the reserved car. The whistle blew. Slowly the train clanged into motion. Frozen into rigidity, Bismarck stood by the window. No muscle in his wrinkled face moved when he heard a few isolated shouts, "Come back soon." One last time his icy gaze swept the jam-packed platform. "A first-class funeral," he murmured to no one in particular.

The destination was Friedrichsruh. Now Bismarck had all the time he could possibly want to enjoy his tall pine trees and breathe the invigorating air of the North German plain. He had often maintained that this was what he preferred to politicking, though few had believed him. Every afternoon he rode on horseback or took long walks, and after his strength had waned, he had himself driven in his landau along the rural roads and through the tiny hamlets. Often he stopped to chat with foresters and innkeepers. He listened to the plaints of the peasants and patted the heads of their flaxen-haired children. Within the boundary lines of his sizable estates, he was still king, but it was a kingdom far too confining for the reach of his spirit.

The manor house was ugly and primitive. It had once been a country inn, and its sixty rooms must have seen a lot of coming and going. House guests were surprised that such a famous person would live with so little refinement and be satisfied in such untidy surroundings.

Bismarck's taste in art ran to pictures of his favorite horse. The giant dogs roamed all over the house or slept sprawled over the stained carpets. Mealtimes were irregular, and the master of the house appeared usually clad in an old dressing gown.

Herbert von Bismarck had followed his father into retirement. True to his eternal role as the obedient son, he voiced no objection when the departing Chancellor declared, "When a man is convinced that a vessel will founder, he doesn't entrust to it the safety of his son." A tyrannical parent broke Herbert's career as he had once thwarted his love.

But if Bismarck had hoped to have Herbert hover about him continuous, he was mistaken. Neither son had much desire to share the country life at Friedrichsruh. They stayed away as often and as long as they dared.

Only Frau Johanna was happy as she bustled from room to room. Now the shriveled woman in those shapeless dresses had her beloved Otto all to herself. From morning to evening she could tend to his comforts, which she did with never faltering devotion.

At first the house was always filled with visitors. They came from every corner of Europe and from as far away as Arabia and China. Correspondents wanted interviews, politicians advice, and historians hoped for factual information. Every time the train stopped at the tiny station, necks craned through the windows. Passengers hoped that, by a stroke of luck, they might get a glimpse of the grand old man. Tourists roamed the village and parked themselves in its beer-garden. Hawkers made good profits with Bismarck pictures and other souvenirs.

Veterans' organizations and bowling associations organized excursions to Friedrichsruh. Glee clubs serenaded the Prince by the light of smoky torches. From Hamburg, some twenty miles away, came school children with their teachers to gaze at the most outstanding exhibit the area had to offer.

A veritable Bismarck cult spread over the whole nation. No town wanted to be without its Bismarckstrasse. Hundreds of monuments rose from town squares, all with the famed spiked helmet pointing skyward.

But nothing corrodes public interest more than the passing of time. As the years rolled by, it became quiet around Friedrichsruh. The mood of its proprietor turned sour. Only one emotion burned undiminished in the huge, now slowly deteriorating body. It was the flame of hate. Gone was the power to destroy those who stood in his way. But he could still attack and wound.

The *Hamburger Nachrichten,* a well-known newspaper, invited Bismarck to become a contributor. Its pages were put at his disposal without any restriction as to space or topic. The offer was accepted with relish. In one year alone, the Hamburg paper printed over a hundred articles under the Bismarck byline. Other publications followed with similar offers. To have a contributor of that renown was, of course, a unique windfall. Circulations rose to a fantastic height, and the wizened journalist seemed to grow younger as he exposed himself again to the tangy breeze of controversy.

He who had once ruthlessly suppressed unfavorable utterings of the press, now attacked the Emperor and his policy-makers with glee. Those on the receiving end were highly embarrassed, but powerless. One could hardly censure a Bismarck or set the police upon him. All the frustrated officials could do was caution foreign governments not to pay any attention to the rantings of a helpless old man. But the readers immensely enjoyed the running feud between the government and its former chief.

With the deftness of a surgeon and with the cruelty of an executioner, the statesman turned political commentator probed into the weaknesses of the existing regime. He kept himself well informed on new developments, and his background knowledge was obviously second to none.

Wherever he looked he saw danger, lack of foresight, bungling. Germany's old ties with England and Russia were becoming frayed, while Paris was wooing St. Petersburg. This was a dangerous courtship. Bismarck had tried very hard to exorcise the grim ghost of the two-front war. Now it was haunting the empire again. The overambitious sovereign was building a new German war fleet, much to the annoyance of England. Bismarck considered the battleships dangerous toys. The strongest foundation of Germany's safety lay in a sensible diplomacy backed by a strong land army. A ruler trying to compete with England on the sea or provoking a clash with Russia was inviting disaster.

Nobody doubted that Bismarck would sooner or later write his memoirs. All the great and near-great have that craving to compose their own obituary. They want to give posterity their personal version of what they had done and what had been done to them. The reminiscences of the Iron Chancellor promised to be especially rich and sensational. Longer than most crowned or uncrowned rulers had he stood at the fulcrum of power. He knew every important personality. He had been a party to every decisive event. His memory could produce intimate details which otherwise would remain buried forever in countless secret files.

From the Cotta Publishing House came the staggering offer of 600,000 marks for an autobiography in six volumes. Bismarck accepted. Several hours a day were set aside for dictation to Lothar Bucher, a former confidential aide at the Foreign Office. This solitary bachelor was one of those individuals who could submerge themselves completely in the service of somebody else. He was perfectly satisfied to be the extended hand of his master. At Friedrichsruh he became singularly useful, since he was one of the few men in his day who had mastered shorthand.

After the breakfast dishes were cleared away, the two old men sat down to their work. Bucher's fingers moved speedily over the sheets as the Prince spluttered out sentences in quick bursts followed by long periods of silence. Often his temper got in the way of his logic. He would rush up and down and shout invectives against invisible adversaries, so that Bucher had a most trying time keeping some sort of order in the manuscript. Or else Bismarck would lapse into soundless reveries while his literary handyman waited patiently with the blank paper before him.

Only two volumes resulted from this collaboration. They were published under the title *Thoughts and Memories*. Then Bucher died, and his employer lost all interest in further literary efforts. It would be naïve to take those reminiscences as straight fact. Despite Bucher's attempts to bring continuity and accuracy into the shapeless narration, it has remained mainly a record of Bismarck's opinions and prejudices. Even the dates mentioned are often false. There was never any attempt to state the other side in a controversy. Facts which reflected unfavorably on the author were altered or simply omitted.

When the narrative reached the crisis of the Spanish succession which was the prelude to the Franco-Prussian War, Bismarck denied the authorship of some letters which would have proven that he had himself stirred up the whole fuss.

He argued with Bucher. "I never wrote such letters. You must be mistaken."

"But I delivered two myself. You sent me to Spain with them."

Even so, the letters did not find their way into the memoirs.

The wars he had engineered were blamed on the aggressiveness of the enemy. The victories were the results of God's judgment.

With bitterness he dwelled on the circumstances surrounding his dismissal. This was not the factual statement of an eyewitness; it was the passionate plea for a verdict of guilty by the prosecutor. "We were turned out like thieves," he wrote, "and lost many possessions by the haste of packing."

That the two volumes became best-sellers was not only due to the author's prominence. They sparkled with fascinating vignettes, and their language was light and elegant. Bismarck was undoubtedly a gifted writer.

The last years of this long life were no more than a prolonged dying. Night was closing in on the Iron Chancellor. Moltke and Roon were dead. Most of the men were gone who had accompanied him for a stretch on his comet-like sweep over the political horizon. Gone were also the women who had loved him: Marie, Cathy and now Johanna. His wife passed away in 1894 after long physical suffering. Though his marriage had not resulted from a burning passion, he had come to depend on her selfless devotion. The gap she left could not be filled anymore.

The occasional visitor now found the Prince sitting motionless in a wheelchair. His shrunken body was wrapped in blankets. A fur cap covered his bald skull. The chalk-white face twitched with neuralgic pains for which Dr. Schweninger knew no cure. All he could do was administer shots of morphine to ease the suffering. Now a professor and a well-known clinical authority, the physician still made regular trips to Friedrichsruh. As he had done for many years, he kept close watch over the patient's daily routine of eating and exercise. When he was absent, a young assistant took his place.

The Emperor made several gestures of reconciliation. Not that he felt any remorse for having fired Bismarck, but he thought it would look better if he and the famous ex-Chancellor were at least on speaking terms.

Unexpected he called at Friedrichsruh and stayed for lunch. The conversation was polite, but it never progressed above the level of military anecdotes and other trivia. Everybody felt uncomfortable at this forced affair. The general feeling was similar when William II bestowed special honors on the retired statesman on the occasion of his eightieth birthday. Characteristically the Emperor sent a life-size portrait of himself. He also appeared in person at the head of a cavalry squadron. From the saddle he delivered a flowery speech of congratulation, excessively extolling the man whom he had sent packing. Bismarck, who could not mount a horse anymore, stood impatiently before his shouting sovereign. He raised his arm in a stiff military salute, but made no answering remarks.

In the summer of 1898, the Emperor was cruising in his big white yacht off the Norwegian coast. When they dropped anchor at the port of Bergen, a telegram announced Bismarck's death. William cabled the family to be sure and await his presence at the funeral.

From the railroad stop he walked the short distance to the house, followed by a bevy of generals and admirals. The relatives of the deceased greeted him with cold formality. Foresters of the Bismarck estate carried the huge black casket to the small village church. They were flanked by two rows of dismounted cavalry. The family saw to it that none but Bismarck retainers touched the coffin. The service was simple and brief. Again coldly formal salutes, and the Emperor was back at his waiting train. Only half an hour had elapsed since his arrival.

The small mausoleum at Friedrichsruh bears the inscription which the landlord himself had composed:

HERE LIES PRINCE BISMARCK
A FAITHFUL SERVANT OF EMPEROR WILLIAM THE FIRST

That was all. No mention of any other emperor. The omission spoke louder than any words could have.

Since then, the controversy around Otto von Bismarck has never ceased. When Germany was riding the crest of success, he was claimed as the nation's model and inspiration. When she brought horror and ruin upon herself and the world, biographers blamed him for having left a heritage of merciless force.

For him politics had indeed been a ruthless sport with winning as the only purpose, with rules observed only when it was advantageous to do so. He kept the peace only by playing an incredibly complex game of diplomatic acrobatics. Once General Caprivi, his successor in the chancery, came for a visit. When Bismarck criticized the current efforts of the German government, Caprivi answered, "Your Serene Highness could keep five balls in the air at one time.

We common mortals cannot juggle so masterfully. We must be content if we can play with one."

A policy built on the peculiar ability of one man cannot endure long. Watching helplessly from the sidelines, Bismarck himself observed the beginning erosion of his system. Within twenty years after his death, the dreaded two-front war had become a reality. In Versailles, scene of his glorious triumph, a defeated Germany had to bow before stern victors who could claim to have applied a lesson taken from his own text.

Still two decades later, the nation was pulled down to the deepest level of barbarism by a maniac who also claimed to be Bismarck's heir. The rule of Adolf Hitler ended with the destruction of everything the Iron Chancellor had built.

Partially at least, he must shoulder the blame. Though he opposed the irresponsible ways of William II and would certainly have recoiled in disgust from the rantings of a Hitler, he helped prepare the scene for their appearance. He made ruthlessness a virtue. He taught the Germans that the state took precedence over the individual, that unquestioning obedience was the first duty of the citizen.

Bismarck's reliance on armed strength encouraged the kind of militarism which sees naked brutality as the only solution to any kind of problem. His policies encouraged Germans to raise arrogant nationalism to the level of a religion. Since the rank and file were excluded from any responsible participation in the government, the stage was set for the entrance of a dictator. An atmosphere of self-centered materialism was created which stilled the voice of the thinker and the spiritual leader.

Yet the fact remains that the Age of Bismarck was an age of peace. Probably no other man could have kept the guns silent from 1870 to 1914. This was a blessing for which almost no price could have been too high.

The judges of Bismarck's record must not fail to consider his wise moderation in the face of strong temptation. Other men of power tried to conquer the whole world and failed. He knew when to stop. Having assured Germany's role as a major power, he was content and refused to engage in further adventures. He streamlined the German nation into an efficient organization. If the citizens of the new empire did not receive democracy, they at least enjoyed a long period of economic progress and of order. In contrast, France, the neighbor and rival, saw forty different cabinets come and fall while Bismarck controlled Germany's destiny.

In whatever field it may be, man stands in awe before the work of the genius. A great man is not necessarily one who commands our love or whom we would want to imitate. But he does evoke our admiration and makes the study of his life a fascinating venture.

CHRONOLOGICAL TABLE OF BISMARCK'S LIFE AND TIMES

1815	Otto von Bismarck born on April 1
	Final defeat of Napoleon
	Congress of Vienna
1822	Otto enrolled in the *Plamannsche Anstalt* in Berlin
1827	Sister Malwine born
1832	Bismarck enrolls at the University of Göttingen
1836	Trial judge in Aachen
1839	Death of Bismarck's mother
	Bismarck moves to the Kniephof
1845	Death of Bismarck's father
	He becomes a member of the Pomeranian provincial Diet
1847	Bismarck becomes a member of the Prussian Diet
	Marriage to Johanna von Puttkamer
1848	Revolutions in several European countries
	Frankfort Parliament
	Birth of daughter Maria
1849	Birth of son Herbert
1851	Bismarck appointed ambassador to the German Federal Diet in Frankfort
1852	Birth of son Bill
1854–56	Crimean War
1858	Prince William becomes regent of Prussia
1859	Bismarck appointed envoy to St. Petersburg
	War of France and Sardinia against Austria
1861	Death of King Frederick William IV of Prussia
	William I becomes King of Prussia

1862	Bismarck appointed ambassador to Paris
	Bismarck named Prime Minister and Foreign Minister of Prussia
	"Blood and Iron" speech
1862–63	Contact with Ferdinand Lassalle
1863	Polish insurrection
1864	War with Denmark
1865	Bismarck becomes a count
1866	War with Austria
1867	North German Confederation; Bismarck becomes its Chancellor
	Bismarck buys the estate of Varzin
1870–71	Franco-Prussian War
1871	Proclamation of the German Empire; Bismarck becomes its Chancellor
1873	The *Kulturkampf* begins
1878	Antisocialist Law
	Congress of Berlin
1882	Triple Alliance (Germany-Austria-Italy)
1887	Reinsurance Treaty with Russia
1888	Death of William I
	Frederick III becomes Emperor
	Death of Frederick III
	William II becomes Emperor
1890	Bismarck resigns
	Bismarck retires to Friedrichsruh
1894	Death of Princess Johanna von Bismarck
1895	Bismarck's eightieth birthday
1898	Death of Otto von Bismarck on July 30

SUGGESTIONS FOR
FURTHER READING

FOR AN INTENSIVE STUDY OF BISMARCK IT IS ALMOST NECESSARY TO
have a reading knowledge of the German language, since much of the
material by and about him has never been translated. This is especially
true of *Bismarck's Collected Works* in eighteen volumes. The following is a sampling of the reading material available in the English
language.

A. BISMARCK'S SPOKEN AND WRITTEN WORD

Bismarck. The Man and the Statesman.   2 vols., New York, Harper,
　1898.
Bismarck. Memoirs.   New York, Fertig, 1967.
Bismarck's Table Talk.   Philadelphia, Lippincott, 1895.
Correspondence of William I and Bismarck.   2 vols., London, 1903.
*The Kaiser vs. Bismarck: Suppressed Letters by the Kaiser and New
　Chapters from the Autobiography of the Iron Chancellor.*   New
　York, Harper, 1921.
Letters.   New York, Scribner, 1878.
Love Letters.   New York, Harper, 1901.

B. BOOKS ABOUT BISMARCK'S LIFE AND TIMES

Cambridge Modern History.   Cambridge University Press, vol. 10,
　1960, vol. 11, 1962.
Carr, Albert.   *Men of Power.* New York, Viking, 1940.

Craig, Gordon. *From Bismarck to Adenauer.* Baltimore, Johns Hopkins University Press, 1958.

Dill, Marshall. *Germany: A Modern History.* Ann Arbor, University of Michigan Press, 1961.

Eyck, Erich. *Bismarck and the German Empire.* New York, Norton, 1958.

Gooch, G. P. *Catherine the Great and Other Studies.* London, Longmans, Green & Co., 1954.

Gooch, G. P. *Studies in German History.* London, Longmans, Green & Co., 1949.

Hamerow, Theodore S., ed. *Otto von Bismarck. A Historical Assessment.* Boston, Heath, 1962.

Kohn, Hans. *The Mind of Germany.* New York, Scribner, 1960.

Ludwig, Emil. *Bismarck.* London, Little, Brown & Co., 1927.

Ludwig, Emil. *Bismarck: the Trilogy of a Fighter* (drama). New York, Putnam, 1927.

Medlicott, W. N. *Bismarck, Gladstone and the Concert of Europe.* New York, De Graff, 1957.

Medlicott, Wilhelm N. *Bismarck and Modern Germany.* Mystic, Conn., Verry, 1965.

Morrow, Ian F. D. *Bismarck* (Great Lives Series). London, Duckworth, 1943.

Novak, K. F. *Kaiser and Chancellor.* New York, Macmillan, 1930.

Pflanze, Otto. *Bismarck and the Development of Germany.* Princeton, N.J., Princeton University Press, 1963.

Pinson, Koppel S. *Modern Germany.* New York, Macmillan, 1954.

Richter, Werner. *Bismarck.* New York, Putnam, 1965.

Snyder, Louis L. *The Blood and Iron Chancellor.* Princeton, N.J., Van Nostrand, 1967.

Taylor, A. J. P. *Bismarck, The Man and the Statesman.* New York, Knopf, 1955.

White, Andrew Dickson. *Seven Great Statesmen.* Garden City, N.Y., Garden City Publ. Co., 1926.

INDEX

ABOUT THE AUTHOR

ALFRED APSLER was born in Vienna, Austria, in 1907 and is now an American citizen. He began writing in his student years, and has been a contributor to newspapers and magazines in Europe and the United States and author of trade books and textbooks. Since 1943 he has taught in high schools and colleges in Oregon and Washington. At present he is Chairman of the Social Science Division of Clark College in Vancouver, Washington, where he lives with his wife. His two children attend universities on the West Coast.